DIVORCING MOM

Divorcing Mom

A MEMOIR OF PSYCHOANALYSIS

MELISSA KNOX

WITH A FOREWORD BY JEFFREY MOUSSAIEFF MASSON

CYNREN

PUBLISHED BY CYNREN PRESS
101 Lindenwood Drive, Suite 225
Malvern, Pennsylvania 19355 USA
http://www.cynren.com/

Printed in the United States of America on acid-free paper

ISBN-13: 978-1-947976-05-4 (hbk)
ISBN-13: 978-1-947976-06-1 (pbk)
ISBN-13: 978-1-947976-07-8 (ebk)

Library of Congress Control Number: 2018934312

The epigraph in chapter 2 is from THE LION, THE WITCH AND THE WARDROBE by C.S. Lewis, copyright © 1950 by C.S. Lewis Pte. Ltd. Reprinted with permission. A version of chapter 2 was previously published as "Through the Wardrobe," *Brain, Child: The Magazine for Thinking Mothers,* originally published August 15, 2015, https://www.brainchildmag.com/2018/04/through-the-wardrobe/. Portions of chapter 3 and other parts of the book were previously published as "The Gods" in *The Wax Paper* 2, no. 1 (2017), http://thewaxpaper.com/. A version of chapter 4 was previously published as "The Intervention," *Gravel,* February 2014, https://www.gravelmag.com/melissa-knox.html. Quotations from A. S. Neill in chapter 6 are reprinted with permision of the copyright holder. Portions of chapter 20 were originally published as "A Whale of a Gift" in *Concho River Review,* Spring/Summer 2018. Lyrics from Rosie Vela, "Fool's Paradise," are reprinted with permission of the copyright holder. The epigraph in chapter 22 is from AMERICAN PASTORAL by Philip Roth. Copyright © 1997 by Philip Roth. Reprinted by permission of Houghton Mifflin Harcourt Publishing Company. All rights reserved.

Every effort has been made to trace the ownership of copyrighted material. Information that will enable the publisher to rectify any error or omission in subsequent reprints will be welcome. In such cases, please contact the publisher at press@cynren.com.

The author has re-created events, locales, and conversations from her memories of them and from personal journals. To maintain their anonymity, in some instances, the author has changed the names of individuals and places. She may have changed some identifying characteristics and details, such as physical properties, occupations, and places of residence.

COVER DESIGN BY Emma Hall

for Josef,
love of my life

We shall overcome.

ZILPHIA HORTON

CONTENTS

FOREWORD

Divorcing Mom is a testament to the authoritarianism inherent in psychoanalysis, the routine brainwashing and gaslighting defining a form of treatment that has more in common with religion than therapy (but let us not forget that Freud called analysis "the impossible profession," without explaining what he meant by this).

Melissa Knox confirms the findings of my three books on psychoanalysis: the first was called *The Assault on Truth,* the truth to which I was referring being sexual abuse of children. I had been trained as a classical Freudian analyst and was told by my instructors that sexual abuse was a common fantasy among women patients. It was what they called a "hysterical lie," meaning that the woman wished it had happened and therefore imagined it and projected it upon her innocent male protagonist (father, brother, uncle, neighbor, friend—but almost never a stranger). I found this hard to swallow; Freud had originally, in 1896, believed women's recollections of abuse, but then he abandoned this belief when he "discovered" the Oedipus complex, the theory that all children experience erotic impulses, especially toward the parent of the opposite sex.

When I met Anna Freud, Freud's daughter, in London back in the 1970s, I told her I thought her father had been wrong to conclude that women imagined seduction rather than actually experiencing it. She did not agree, but she did allow me to examine her father's letters to his best friend, Wilhelm Fliess. I was convinced I would find corroborating evidence that the history of Freud's abandonment of his initial belief was far more complex and nuanced than we had been led to believe. I was right. And that was *The Assault on Truth*. That work was one of discovering documents (unpublished letters, accounts from the Paris Morgue, and so on).

After *The Assault on Truth* was published in 1984, I received a large number of letters from women who had been or were in psychoanalysis with orthodox Freudians, and they were relieved that at last a male psychoanalyst believed them and did not ascribe their experiences to fantasy. These letters told stories remarkably similar to the story you'll read in the book you are holding in your hands.

My next book was far more personal: *Final Analysis*. It, too, seems to mirror Knox's story. We both had analysts who appeared to be completely unhinged. I named my analyst, Irvine Schiffer, who threatened to sue me. He admitted that what I said was true. He just worried that it would or had already adversely affected his practice. A single bad apple, or perhaps just two? I doubted that at the time; after all, I had been in exalted places, as director of the Freud Archives, and knew many analysts quite well. Few of them came off well, and so this led me to examine an even larger topic: whether the very idea of psychotherapy in general, be it Freudian, Jungian, Rogerian, Gestalt, group, Laingian, or any other, would be an improvement on ordinary friendship. The answer was clear: *no*. And so came my final book in the trilogy, *Against Therapy*.

It is at this point that Knox and I part company. She is more generous than I and more willing to give therapists the benefit of the doubt, especially those she doesn't know. (She pulls no punches when it comes to her own fatally flawed analyst. He behaved more like a cranky, eccentric, unlovable uncle with incestuous tendencies barely kept in check.)

When I read her chapter on how her analyst, Oscar Sternbach, confronted—or declined to confront—the incest in her family, I asked Knox what Sternbach had actually said: had he denied the abuse entirely? I was interested, because I had seen this story before; in fact, it was the very cornerstone of my research into Freud's views on child sexual abuse.

Knox replied that he'd talked out of both sides of his mouth. He had agreed that her father sexually abused her. In some sessions he insisted that she'd wanted to seduce her father, in others that the seductions were not her fault because she was under the age of seven at the time the abuse started. In response to the story of her grandfather's sexual abuse of her mother, Sternbach asked, "So what?" Yes, it had happened, he added, but, with a shrug, "You opened a closet. You saw a ghost." And, he made clear, Knox should never have told anyone in her family—she should only have talked to him, the analyst. No, she should not write about this, should not write about her grandfather's strange relationship with his daughters or with a model who became an American prophetess of incest and its consequences, namely, Anaïs Nin. "Forget about it," Sternbach sneered. "One doesn't say these things about one's family. You are an idiot." At this point, Knox went home, opened a window in her sixth-floor apartment, and leaned out, as she told me, "almost too far." Yes, his antiquated (but common) conservative views nearly drove to suicide a very talented woman with the right instincts and a refusal to obfuscate the truth. Nice one, Sternbach.

Here we see what I came to identify as the most pressing problem of therapy: the therapist substitutes his or her view of the world for that of the patient or client. Of course, no one ever admits to doing this: "we are simply bringing to the surface the hidden views of the person on the couch," they maintain. If only. (And, to be fair, that must happen from time to time. But who knows how common it is, as we never get to witness what goes on in that secluded space?)

Divorcing Mom drives home that Oscar Sternbach, like many analysts, had no interest in Knox's reality. Perhaps he lacked the intellectual wherewithal to grasp it. Instead, he substituted his own goal, to control her, which manifested in his assertion— did he actually have the arrogance to believe this?—that "I am the only one who can help you," and he claimed the authority, *in loco parentis,* to "bring you up," because her parents were not competent to do so. Do I need to persuade you from this excerpt? Clearly he wasn't listening to Knox, or he didn't care.

Or his own needs took precedence over anything else: Knox and her mother, both, had to love *him*. His group sessions were all pointing in the same direction: love me, admire me, adore me. He thought of himself as Freud's best student (not that they ever met). I knew Freud (Anna, at least). He was no Freud.

Knox's father was fair game—he was competition for Sternbach's authority, and Sternbach wanted to be the only voice in Knox's life.

Reeducation is something Freud *in theory* shied away from, but in practice, I cannot see how any therapist can avoid the trap. "Be more like me" is the hidden agenda. It was possible for Freud to criticize parents for the short time he believed the women who told him about abuse: their fathers, after all, were criminals. But once Freud "abandoned" that true view, he had to take the side of the parents: the children were imagining terrible crimes by their fathers (or, more rarely, by their mothers), who only meant the best for them—and this is the thanks they got. For Sternbach, Knox's mother, who paid for the psychoanalysis, could do no wrong, as the following exchange from *Divorcing Mom* reveals. Fourteen-year-old Knox is describing her mother's odd behavior: "If you were a drunk lying on your side with a few flies buzzing over your smelly body, my mother would love you. She would find you and she would love you. You'd be sleeping peacefully in a subway car, and she'd come up from behind, tap you somewhere inappropriate, and say, 'Oh? Excuse me? Do you need anything?' Sometimes she held out a dollar bill or a chocolate bar, and cheered, as if for a favorite team, when it was accepted." Knox mentions her mother doing chorus girl kicks on Broadway, apparently to get attention from passersby. Sternbach replies, "Do you *know* why you dislike your mother?" Knox is puzzled:

> I sat up on the couch and twisted my head around to see his expression, which looked ominous. I felt thrust off-balance. He seemed to be saying there was something I had missed about why I disliked my mother. But I thought I knew that: she expected me to admire or reassure her all the time, liked to pretend that she was the little girl and I was the mean

mother—I was just getting warmed up talking about how she couldn't cook, let my father—

Dr. Sternbach interrupted me.

"Do you *know* why?" he repeated.

I fell silent, since he wanted another answer, and I didn't have it.

"Because you are so dependent on her!"

Knox is stunned—she wishes she had a mother on whom she could depend, and now her analyst is telling her she's already too dependent on the one she's got. He drives home the message:

"Your mother is *generous*! You have no idea what it is to have children, to care for them. No idea at all."

I had nothing to say. That was true—I had no idea about being a mother.

"You are spoiled! A terrible child. You should be grateful to your mother for all she has done for you."

"But . . . she's, somehow, so childish." I braced myself. The fist slammed down again, right by my ear.

"So she's childish!"

I sat up again.

Dr. Sternbach cast me an exasperated look, tapped on the arm of his La-Z-Boy.

"Don't you see that you *must* have a good relationship with your mother? Otherwise *you will not be able to have good relationships at all.* If you cannot build a relationship with her, you cannot build *any* relationships. You want friends, you want boyfriends. Well, start at home—with your mother."

"But she doesn't listen—she does all kinds of strange things."

"You are an idiot! Like most teenagers, you think only of yourself. You don't think what your mother goes through or what she feels."

Thump! Thump! His fist hit the couch. He sounded absolutely sure of himself, and I saw that my bad relationship with Mom was my fault, that if I didn't fix the problem, I'd never have a relationship with a boy or anyone else. I hoped desperately there might be some way around this problem. Dr. Sternbach was muttering under his breath.

"Spoiled!" he said, so that I could hear him. "You are just a spoiled brat."

Well, in the scheme of things, this is not the worst a psychoanalyst has said, but it's right up there. Sternbach was not thinking of the girl on his couch but of his own views about children, about the world, about mothers, about families. He was completely hemmed in, stumped. Naturally, he could not admit to this; indeed, he could not even imagine this possibility. In his view, he was right, always. He had no capacity to see beyond himself. Worse than mansplaining was this insistence on wisdom from a man of little brains.

Her mother's intrusiveness, inappropriate remarks, gestures, behaviors, were things Knox was not allowed to bring up; if she did, Sternbach yelled and made comments like "So your mother's childish! It's amazing she's survived her marriage!" or, balefully, "Your mother will always help you." Over and over, the same note sounded: the mother was good and the daughter was bad, ungrateful. Clearly Sternbach identified with Knox's parents rather than with the child she had been. I am not surprised. His own behavior was abusive: telling her she wanted him to spank her and wondering if he should. This borders on malpractice.

Sternbach was never censored by his peers. Did they have any idea what he did? (It is unlikely they even knew. Another problem: psychoanalysis takes place in private—hardly anyone beyond the patient knows what goes on there.) He practiced successfully for many years. An award is named after him. Had he been an electrician, he probably would have been stopped long ago.

"OK," I can hear someone say, "so he was a terrible analyst, or psychologist. We grant this. But does this reflect on the profession as a whole? Should we generalize from one bad analyst to an entire profession with thousands of practitioners over the years who have helped hundreds of thousands of people?" Well, I would answer, that's fine in theory. But how can one be certain that the help was genuine? Who is to decide, and at what point? In reality, it would require serious research to determine what results any analysis brings. Meanwhile, this is an account of what it was like to be a young teenager in the thrall of a man old enough to be her grandfather, who offers to spank her and suggests she remove her blouse to get over being "inhibited." Can we say that Sternbach's way of doing things undermines the enterprise of psychoanalysis as a whole? Possibly not. But it is a clear indication of the dangers inherent in any therapy—especially where a young girl or woman is seeing a male therapist. You just never know what goes on in the therapist's head and what liberties he might take when he feels he is the king of his own castle.

Not only is *Divorcing Mom* more grist for my mill; it is also a cracking good read.

JEFFREY MOUSSAIEFF MASSON, August 2018

Prologue

Why did the narcissist cross the road?
She thought it was a boundary.

She wanted me slaughtered. By a young butcher, preferably a sadistic one, who would hack me into chunks, salt me, and stow me in his downstairs freezer. Then she could wail tragically, launching her arms and contracting her abdomen with the drama of Martha Graham dancing Clytemnestra. Relatives, friends, and perfect strangers would come from miles around to grieve with the woman whose daughter was so brutally taken from her. The *New York Times* would headline the event—she'd get her picture in the paper.

I imagined her drooling at the thought.

After garnering lots of sympathy at the funeral, she'd want me revived. She'd love to see me walk down the aisle with a handsome son-in-law—*her* handsome son-in-law—as long as heads turned to look at her dress instead of mine.

None of these thoughts made themselves into words when Josef asked what my mother wanted for me. I told the first white lie of our relationship: "Oh, she just wants my happiness."

I was forty. Josef and I were enjoying a warm afternoon in April and had just gotten engaged. A Peter Pan bus was rolling us toward a Nantucket vacation. We pulled out of the yellowish-tiled Holland Tunnel.

STAY IN LANE said the bright neon sign by the tunnel.

Forget that. I'd switched my lane for good. A lifelong New Yorker, I was dreaming of Josef's—soon to be our—patio in the heart of Bavaria. The grape arbor in his garden. The balcony with a view of grassy, rolling hills. In the distance, the Frauen-bergkapelle, a pretty white baroque chapel.

Thinking how different, in just a few months, my world would be, I looked out at white lines on the dark tarmac, green signs on an unscenic I-95.

THRU TRAFFIC. I knew where I was going.

EXIT. I was definitely getting out of New York. My past, my city, my world. In the years to come, as Josef and I sat eating dinner and watching TV, the chirps of sparrows and barks of dogs filtering in from outside, he would say, "I'm glad I got you out of there." Sometimes I sulked, wishing I could grab a *New York Times* and a coffee in a paper cup with Greek columns on it and hop on the downtown local. I missed the rattle of the subway, the traffic noises. I still miss the subway and the places it took me, but I am truly glad he got me out of there.

Leaning back on the rough, plush seats, we held hands, and then Josef pulled out an envelope of photos of his family. I flipped through images of his brother on a tractor in front of the Bavarian farm, his towheaded toddler nephew chasing hens, his sister-in-law brandishing a gigantic, creamy-icinged cake.

"Do you like organically fed lamb?" Josef asked. "I know a young shepherd who could slaughter a lamb for us."

"Wow!" I'd love it if he'd have a lamb butchered just for the two of us.

Maybe for the three of us.

A third member of our family was, I believed, already growing inside me. Meanwhile, I'd cover the lamb in fresh rosemary and garlic. Roast some potatoes.

"I have a big downstairs freezer," Josef said. "We can store whatever we don't eat."

I could almost smell the aroma of roasting lamb as I imagined place settings lit by Bavarian sunsets. How I'd enjoy bustling around the kitchen—so much roomier than my tiny New York one—steaming some broccoli to go with the lamb. Or maybe green beans. Would we drink Bordeaux or Beaujolais with our freshly butchered lamb? Could we get those wines in Bavaria, or only beer?

It was then that Josef looked at me sideways and inquired, "What does your *mother* want for you?"

Sidestepping that, I asked about his mother.

"I was very happy with the mother I had," he said.

In photos, his mother's warm blue eyes—identical to his, trained delightedly on him and his brothers—speak volumes about her loving, traditionally maternal character. But she'd turn in her grave if she knew I wasn't Catholic—not even a believer. She is said to have waved a pitchfork at a Protestant female friend of Josef's, warning that no non-Catholic would marry her boy. Someone with his experiences of a protective mother who baked cakes and made Bavarian *Dampfnudeln* would find my mother unbelievable. His head would spin.

I could easily imagine Mom waving a pitchfork, sprouting horns, and swishing a tail—while admiring herself in the mirror, pulling me over so I could tell her how fabulous she looked. She could barely tell one religion from another, a trait I shared. I didn't tell Josef any of this.

ONE

The Spider and the Fly

"Will you walk into my parlor?" said the Spider to the Fly,
'Tis the prettiest little parlor that ever you did spy;
The way into my parlor is up a winding stair,
And I've a many curious things to show when you are there."

"Oh no, no," said the little Fly, "to ask me is in vain,
For who goes up your winding stair
—can ne'er come down again."

MARY HOWITT, "The Spider and the Fly"

M y mamma used to read me this."
A smile ghosted Dad's lips, his southern lilt deepening.
A dreamy look gleamed in his eyes, the humid summer evening
settling, a sleeping animal before a storm.

Dad sat in the kitchen where we could look out at the Hudson
River, the sun sinking below the trees in Riverside Park. A lone
fly circled the lightbulb. The air, New York August, stayed hot
and steamy even though both kitchen windows remained wide
open. Dad hummed, nodded—the lack of a breeze relaxing the
hand around his drink, his glass beaded with condensation.

Across the river on the New Jersey side, neon lights started
glittering—Palisades Amusement Park lit up. Wild greens, deep

pinks, flickering blues, whirled on strange machines and were reflected in the waters of the Hudson.

Dad smelled of Vitalis and gin; he had lots of hair on his chest and legs. We were alone. At last. I climbed into his lap, looked at the pictures in his book. In my favorite illustration, a dapper fly in a monocle, tremulous as Little Red Riding Hood, tips his hat to a hairy, potbellied spider sporting an axe like a codpiece. Eyes trained on the fly, the spider smiles: *Such an easy mark!*

Dad grinned as he read, his head wagging to the rhythm. I didn't want to look up when I heard Mom's bare feet striding across the floor, the ice in her orange juice clinking.

"*Must* you?" Mom glared, arching her eyebrows. Her face pale with fatigue, she let him know she found the spider's wheedling, flattering, lying, and trickery, verse after verse after verse, "Disgusting!"

"*Read*, Daddy, *read!*"

What if the two of them fought? He'd shove me off his lap. I gripped his wrists.

Mom wanted that fly rescued, but *immediately!*

Giggling, Dad shifted the chair around so we were facing away from her, held our book up to the light, declaimed,

"I'm sure you must be weary, dear, with soaring up so high.
Will you rest upon my little bed?" said the Spider to the Fly—

I didn't know why he was laughing, but I liked his laugh and the way he was caught up in the story.

"Harry, you'll give her *nightmares!*" Mom said.

"*Daddy!*" I yelled. "*Read!*"

"*Harry!*"

Ignoring Mom, Dad read on:

"There are pretty curtains drawn around; the sheets are fine
and thin,
And if you like to rest a while, I'll snugly tuck you in!"

By this time, Dad was snorting, wiping his nose with the back of his hand, whipping out a cotton handkerchief to mop his hand and face.

"It's brutal! Deceitful!" Mom yelled.

Dad turned our chair back toward her.

"My *mamma* read me this, Celine, and *we* didn't have night-mares!" He looked, for a moment, like a boy pleading with his mother. Mom's face hardened. Dad's expression slid from puzzlement to exasperation. He shook his head, mouth set, and sloshed another jigger into his drink.

I watched Mom walk into the living room, stand by the window facing the George Washington Bridge, and sigh, her eyes cast upward, as if praying. Or crying. Maybe she could find out how sweet his sadness was. Maybe she would come back, sit down beside him. Maybe she would smile. At Daddy.

She didn't. Daddy reached for his drink, let me grab it with both hands, allowing me a sip. The melted ice and gin-flavored tonic slipped down, slightly bubbly, slightly sweet, making me dizzy.

He kept reading as I kept hanging on.

I could see the dark outline of Mommy in the living room. She glanced over her shoulder, as if wondering what Daddy would do if she were to decide to return to the kitchen. I could tell by the way she was standing how much she wanted him to notice she was angry.

When Dad read the part where the spider drags the fly up his winding stair, Mom cringed. When the fly met its fate in the comfort of the spider's master bedroom, Mom stage-whispered, "Oh, *Harry*."

Dad reached for his other book, the one with the torn red cover, pages brown, crumbling a bit at the edges, and opened it. While I gazed at a picture of an upside-down bird, claws extended, an arrow securely anchored in its breast, Dad sang a happy dirge: "Whooo killed Cock Robin? Whoo-ooo-ooo killed Cock Robin?"

My mother put her hands over her ears. Dad's eyes glinted. I bounced, waiting for the next line, which emerged as a gut-wrenching sigh, though I supposed he was one second from collapsing into giggles.

"I, said the Sparr-ah! With mah teensy bow 'n' arrah!"

The more Dad drank, the thicker his accent, the more lugubri-ous his delivery. The question arose: who caught Cock Robin's blood? With a heartrending shudder, Dad gave the answer:

I, said the Fish
With my little dish,
I caught his blood.

Dad drew out the last word to three syllables, "bluh—uh—ud,"
snickering as if only the two of us understood.

TWO

Through the Wardrobe

He had a strange, but pleasant little face . . .
and out of the hair there stuck two horns,
one on each side of his forehead.

C. S. LEWIS, *The Lion, the Witch and the Wardrobe*

I am a tomboy," I announced. I was wearing black high-tops, like my younger brother, and OshKosh overalls.

Mom was holding the drawings of big-boobed girls that I'd done with my friend Leslie. Leslie's mom said the drawings were disgusting.

Mom's face shrieked the same message, even though she was an artist and had told me that what Leslie and I were doing was called "life drawing." I'd never shown Mom my drawings. She must have gone into my room.

"These proportions are all wrong. The arms are too long for the body, the head too large . . ."

I squirmed. The drawings were girlie-girlie, but I'd liked them until Mom saw them. I grabbed them and ripped them up.

"I'd rather be a boy."

"Do you have a boy's name?" Mom was wearing a baggy shirt, jeans, and a newsboy's cap.

"It might be Bucky. Maybe Honey, but maybe Bucky."

Lately, getting hit in the chest hurt. I tried hitting myself in the chest, and that hurt, too. Before, it hadn't. If I slammed my fists against my nipples, maybe I wouldn't get breasts. Mom's face—was she going to cry?

While I decided on Honey or Bucky, my mother called Dr. Berkeley.

Mom and I were sitting in the kitchen of a rented house on India Street in Nantucket. I was enjoying the sunset sliding across the widow's walks down the street, drifting off into daydreams of the beach, looking forward to biking to Cisco Beach or Madaket, wondering whether I'd see bayberry bushes along the way, anticipating going to Arno's on Main Street for blueberry pancakes, and hoping that the lady with my favorite chocolate fudge still had her shop.

As I was finishing dinner, Mom explained that Aunt Berkeley had asked her to ask me something. "Do you want to have your vagina cut out and a penis sewn in?" The question shot from my mother's mouth. Her eyes widened in shock, as if someone had just cursed or farted, or both.

"No, Mom," I said, in a please-pass-the-butter voice. I didn't want to imagine someone hacking off a penis and cutting me where it really hurts to attach the thing, but I couldn't get the image out of my head.

My fascination with Dracula and vampires had been growing before she popped her question, and I was a longtime fan of Barnabas Collins, the sensitive vampire in *Dark Shadows,* but Mom's question mobilized my interest.

Early that summer, she'd mentioned how much she'd enjoyed a girl's camp in Vermont.

"When I was your age, I went swimming, I went canoeing, we sang songs—"

"How long does camp last?" I asked. But she was lost in happy reminiscence.

"We made campfires, we climbed mountains, we—"

"*How many weeks?*"

"—roasted marshmallows, we learned archery, we even put on, let me see, which Gilbert and Sullivan? I know I sang—"

"MOM! *How long can I go for?*"

"—the piney air was . . . what?"

"I want to go! How long does the camp last?"

"Oh, well, it's a whole eight weeks, but if you don't want to go that long—"

"I want to go!"

When my summer camp uniform arrived, I opened my closet, pushed my way behind the racks of dresses, the school uniforms, and the coats to the very back, where I tapped the cedar wall and pretended, one last time, that it was melting away, such that I found myself crunching across a winter-white landscape on my way to the faun's house in frost-covered Narnia. I'd practically memorized the chapters in which the White Witch tempts Edmund with magically enhanced Turkish delight, whips out her wand to turn Santa into stone, and finally gets her hash settled by the now-rehabilitated Edmund. I'd tie her to the stone table myself and send an army of ten-foot-tall ogres and rheumy-eyed hags with knives and pitchforks after her. Some of the meaner giants would sharpen the stone knife for me.

My mother sewed in my name tags and then drifted into painting little green trees up the legs and basin of the kitchen sink. She concocted inedible dishes she called "Chinese food" out of several breakfasts' worth of leftover scrambled eggs and a few anemic scallions from the back of the crisper. She needed to talk to my father—right now—as the ice clinked in his second gin and tonic.

I started packing, even though camp wouldn't start for another four weeks. At night, I tried on the uniform and was delighted to find I'd need a belt to hold up the shorts, that the green knee socks could be pulled over my knees, that the hiking boots (L.L. Bean "Ruff-Outs") required Kleenex in the toe for me to be able to walk in them without my feet slipping around until I tripped, and that I'd have to roll the sleeves of my black watch plaid camp shirt up so they didn't flop over my wrists.

These clothes had to fit me for a long time. I was planning to wear them for maybe a year, if I couldn't afford to buy clothes on my own once I made my getaway. I could maybe escape during summer camp or right before my mother picked me up.

I'd need a winter coat, but somewhere down the line I'd find one in some Salvation Army thrift shop. Maybe I could get into an orphanage. I was sure they'd take fifth graders. Or I'd stow away on the Nantucket steamship, pretend to be an orphan, and get adopted by a family on the island.

Or maybe I'd decide to stay. Anything could happen during those eight weeks. By the end of summer camp, some mysterious transformation, fueled entirely by my wishes, might occur. When my parents and brother came to pick me up, they'd look like extras from the set of *Leave It to Beaver*. Or at least they'd resemble *The Addams Family*. I wouldn't even recognize them. My mother would call my father "honey," a word she had never uttered, and even though her voice would be pleasantly low, unlike anything I'd heard at home, I'd know her immediately. My father would smile and bow like Lurch and, also like Lurch, wouldn't speak. My brother, inconspicuous as Wednesday Addams perching demurely in a corner, would sit inertly in the car the whole time my trunk was being loaded and speak a single sotto voce "hello" when I climbed in for the ride home.

Even if none of these things happened, maybe I'd befriend some other camper whose parents had always wanted another daughter, or maybe a sister for their little Clara, yes, a companion for their lonely, sickly child who had a cleft palate. I'd play Heidi and get her up to speed by helping her learn to speak— and to climb every mountain, too. Then they'd have a good excuse to lavish upon me their considerable wealth and lasting affection, and I'd fit right in to their family. It'd be easy. They'd be so grateful to me for saving the child they had almost given up for lost. A whole eight weeks! Yes, anything could happen.

Near the end of our drive to camp, Mom and I stopped at a roadside restaurant for dinner, and I dove into my chicken with gravy and wild rice, eating so quickly I could hardly taste it. Suddenly I—who am so allergic to nuts that in my thirties, a boyfriend's kiss would turn my lips into a red welt after he'd eaten a hazelnut—felt my throat start to swell. I waved at Mom, sitting opposite me, because I could barely speak. The skin on my hands, my arms, got bright red and itchy. Quarter-sized hives were popping out all over. I was scratching like an ape.

"Oh, my goodness, you look tired. We should get you to bed."

"My wild rice gravy has nuts in it."

"Really? Oh, dearie, dearie me. Your throat does sound a bit scratchy. Would you like a little dessert? Or maybe some juice?"

"Mom, I need a doctor."

"A doctor?" she sounded fuzzy, like someone who was just waking up but would rather put her head back down on the pillow.

"I really need one now."

"Oh," she fumed. "Let me see. OK. Wonder if I have enough gas." We got in the car, and she began driving. The car edged forward reluctantly.

"Oh, Melissa, look at the deer!" Mom yelped. "It's so pretty!" She slowed to a crawl and pointed. "Oh, I'd love to paint that! We could stop for a minute."

"Mom, I need a hospital. Please. Right away. Take me to a hospital."

"A hospital? Oh, OK. If you *really* think so." She shook her head. If I could only calm down and notice the countryside, I wouldn't have these problems. She pointed out another deer frolicking through the birch trees.

I saw a state trooper's car on the side of the road and told her to stop and ask him.

"We don't want to bother him, do we? After all—"

"Pull the car over!"

My mother rolled down her window and told the state trooper it was so good of him to chat with us. She hoped it was no bother. Was there a doctor around here or a hospital?

From the back seat, I rapped on my window, said, "Help!"

He turned and saw my face. Urgently, he told Mom to follow his car.

By the time we got to the small local hospital, I could no longer see or walk. I lost consciousness. I woke on a gurney, in my hand an envelope of pink capsules that reminded me of candy. My mother informed me that I had been given a large shot of adrenaline. I had been unconscious for some time, hours, apparently, and she had on her face the look of a child whose parents have arrived two hours late to pick her up. Mom took me to the bed-and-breakfast near the camp, where I spent three days in bed. She read to me and provided stale sandwiches.

Meanwhile, I imagined the plates of homemade blancmange decorated with fresh mint leaves I'd have served up (the way Jo waits on Laurie in *Little Women*) if Clara of the ruined soft palate had been lying where I was, and if I had been a rosy-cheeked Heidi, feeling considerably perkier than I did right then. I relished the ability to breathe but felt shaky whenever I got out of bed. I looked at Mom humming a little tune under her breath and murmuring about what a lovely lake we were on and wouldn't I like to go swimming?

I realized I'd need to check all restaurant food myself carefully from now on. Not to mention learning to cook, something I would do by watching my father, whose love of southern-fried anything dominated our cuisine at home.

A few pounds thinner, I joined my tentmates three days after camp had started. I enjoyed the piney aromas and the quiet.

The counselor introduced the girls, suggesting we all tell what our daddies do.

"My daddy's a bobbin manufacturer," said a pretty redhead with widely spaced eyes. "My daddy says we'll have a fine old time," said the other girl, shy and genteel. "He's a professor."

My father concealed his mini-bottle of Gordon's London Dry Gin in his shirt pocket when our family ate at the Moon Palace restaurant, where we always ordered the same dish, chicken with snow peas. Dad poured the gin into his water glass. When the waiter's back was turned, Dad pocketed a few pieces of cutlery.

I didn't think either of those girls had a dad like mine.

I liked the Chinese restaurant meals, because Dad got such a kick out of snitching the fork and knife, plus not paying for his drink, that he didn't yell or slap anyone. He grabbed my hand on the way home and cried, "You walk with Daddy!"

"I hate my father," I said to the group of camp girls.

The counselor's eyebrows shot up. The shy girl invited me to play cards; the redhead said she loved cheese fondue.

A week after I arrived, the summer camp director sent my mother a letter about "your very articulate young lady." What she meant is that although surrounded by peaceful Vermont lakes and pine trees, I was obsessed with Count Dracula. My tentmates were sick of hearing about how much blood dripped from his teeth. The camp director's letter added that I "burst with ideas" and that I had "so much to offer other children in the way of lively companionship." She meant that instead of engaging in such companionship, I liked to pull the legs off daddy long-legs. I liked to pour salt on slugs. She'd noticed that I preferred hiding under my bed with a flashlight, reading, never learning anyone's name or talking, except while gobbling meals, when I opened my mouth and stories poured out. I talked nonstop at the camp dinner table, where no one ever slapped me and no one had ever been slapped.

When camp ended in late August, my mother came by herself to pick me up. I felt glad she hadn't brought Dad. There wouldn't be fighting in the car. After we returned to New York, my counselor sent my parents a long letter. She wondered whether my "fetish for the bizarre" might be "a substitute for carrying on a relationship" in which I felt uneasy, in other words, that my behavior was "a shell to avoid letting other people know" that I did not "have as much self-confidence as she often shows on the surface." I laughed as my mother, casting me a doleful look, read this out loud. If I could fool my counselor, then I could fool other people, too, and I almost felt a genuine self-confidence.

"What is going on with you?" asked Mom, bursting into tears.

"Melissa talked a great deal about sex, especially at the beginning of the summer," wrote the camp director in her own report at the end of the summer. She seemed astonished. Sex was indeed one of my favorite topics, and I had not been able to stop looking for it everywhere. At camp, I told the other girls about the movie version of *To Sir, with Love,* which none of them had seen. The film version, I told them, didn't use the scene in the book in which a girl throws a used sanitary napkin into the fireplace in a school classroom. Sanitary napkin! Blood! Menstruation! Which has something to do with sex! And I kept harping on this moment with my bemused campmates.

At camp, I felt like an anthropologist visiting an unknown tribe I might like to join, and nothing reassured me more than the sight of other campers laughing at my antics. Stories of Catherine the Great getting crushed by a horse being lowered, for erotic purposes, by crane fascinated me. I told them. Repeatedly.

I pretended to be a vampire. "My name is Count Dracula, and I come to suck your blohhh-huuh-huuhd," I'd say. I thought this was very funny. I said it again and again.

Neither vampires nor sex stories blotted out my most unforgettable moment, the one I kept trying to exfoliate with the energy of a dragon shedding his skin but which followed me everywhere. I thought of it often, and when I did, I tried to shift my attention to my favorite joke, which went like this:

> A young lady is just about to marry. She asks her mother to find her a black lace negligee and fold it carefully into her suitcase. Mom forgets and just packs a pink flannel nightgown. On the wedding night, the groom gets shy, saying he will undress in the bathroom and that the bride should not look. She opens her suitcase, finds the pink flannel nightgown, and cries, "Oh, it's all pink and wrinkly!" The groom yells, "I told you not to look!"

I loved this joke, finding it so amusing that I had to stop and calm myself to be understood when I told it. All pink and wrinkly! Hilarious. I always ended up laughing so hard I could barely tell the joke. Except that the other kids didn't get it or looked shocked.

But always, I remembered most vividly the thing I wanted to forget. My brother was three, I was five, and Daddy was weaving around the room giggling and reeking of Gordon's London Dry Gin. He danced with us. He pointed a finger toward my brother. He sat in front of us and his face was all red, his eyes glassy. He stuck that finger into my brother's face. "No, me, Daddy, *me*!" I cried, jealous. He laughed and said, "Pull my finger!" My brother pulled his finger, and Daddy emitted a long, loud belch.

"Me! Me!"

"Pull my finger, and I'll burp," he promised, and I pulled it. He burped long and loud, and we laughed. But he had to top himself; the finger was just the peanut gallery.

"Come on, kiddies!" he cried jovially. "Watch Daddy pee!" We followed him into the bathroom. He shut and locked the door, because Mom was on the other side of it. We laughed. This was a game, like keep-away. The bathroom had white and black diamond-shaped tiles, and the lights were bright. He pulled out

15

his penis the way a fireman unrolls a hose—he just hand-over-handed it, and it kept on rolling out, more and more, until I almost wondered if that thing would hit the wall. I couldn't see anything else: it was all pink and wrinkly. Then it reared its head like an angry red giant. It was beautiful; it was ugly; it was the tree of the knowledge of pain and pleasure. It was a walk with a faun in the pale moonlight. It was the entire world, and the world was ending. The room disappeared. The thing seemed as thick as my head. A stream of urine loud as a cataract shot into the toilet, enough to drown all New York. You could have gone over the falls in a barrel in that stuff.

My brother and I were the best audience imaginable.

"Wow, Daddy!" I said.

We clapped.

"Wow!" my brother agreed. "Can you do that again, Daddy? Can you do it now?"

Wham! Wham! Wham! We were so agog with these previously hidden talents that only after a moment did I realize that the entire time we'd been in the bathroom, Mom had been pounding on the door and yelling. But we didn't like her. It was Daddy who claimed all our love. When Daddy opened the door, she was still yelling so loud and pounding so hard that she didn't realize it had opened and fell flat on the tiles. I think we stepped over her and ran to our rooms.

Right then, I felt like I was falling off a cliff and my stomach clutched. Within a few years, I started dreaming every night that I was rolling down the hill at 111th Street and my head was going to smash into the black lamppost at the bottom of the hill. I always awoke with a lurch, panting and sweating, every night.

When I started summer camp, I believed that because I was in a new place, surrounded by happy people, people not in my family, I would be allowed to forget everything that went before. I'd get a do-over.

The cedar wall at the back of my closet would dissolve; I'd walk out into a winter wonderland, get invited to tea with a friendly faun, who would lead me back to the lamppost so that I could get home—only unlike Lucy in *The Lion, the Witch and the Wardrobe,* I wouldn't go back home. I'd stay in Narnia.

When Lucy visits the faun in Narnia, he wears a red scarf over his handsome, hairy chest in the Pauline Baynes illustrations. His furred hindquarters conceal his tumescence—for what else is Mr. Tumnus, the faun who takes Lucy back to his cozy den, where he plies her with tea and lulls her into a trance with the honeyed tunes of his flute? The music makes Lucy feel like crying and laughing and dancing and going to sleep. He bursts into tears.

He has been bad, and he's afraid they'll cut off his tail and his horns.

What else would you do with men who seduce little girls?

But Lucy forgives him.

When my father came to my room at night, and he sobbed and stroked me, I pretended to be asleep. I felt like laughing and crying and dancing and sleeping, and I did not want the tune to stop. When he wept, he loved me.

THREE

Gods, Gods!

As flies to wanton boys are we to th' gods.
They kill us for their sport.

WILLIAM SHAKESPEARE, *King Lear*

The school library became my favorite place to forget my third-grade report card, in which Mrs. Trotman had written, "Math is Melissa's Waterloo."

Facing the East River, a worn, flat, pewter-blue linen window seat beneath me, I opened *The Lion, the Witch and the Wardrobe*. The aroma of the cafeteria, with its great steamy, stainless steel pots of creamed chicken and rice, faded. Snow fell around me, and sleigh bells jingled. I wanted to warn Edmund, who was staring and stammering at the White Witch, not to talk to strangers. Face flushed, mouth smeared with Turkish delight, he was revealing—*She's really mean, Edmund!*—the existence of one brother and two sisters. I closed my eyes. *Don't tell her! She's up to something!* I said in my mind.

"Melissa!"

"What!" I looked up. For a moment, the window seat and Mrs. Raudabusch, the gray-haired librarian, came into focus. I closed my mouth with the sensation that I might have been drooling. I willed away her tired, kind face, in my mind holding

Edmund's hand and yanking him away from the cruel queen. Why couldn't he see that witch was lying about having any right to the Narnian throne?

Mrs. Raudabusch was looking at me as if she wondered whether I might be retarded. Many of my teachers did this.

"I'm calling your name and you're closing your eyes at me. That's not polite, dear. I've been saying your name for a few minutes. You should go back to your homeroom now," the librarian said, pointing out that I was late.

Just when I was rescuing Edmund. Just when I was wishing I could open my closet at home and find—instead of the wooden wall—trees, a faun, a wicked witch, and a lion who might *really* save Edmund and kill that witch.

I felt the cool windowpane press against my arm and shivered. Might be an icicle from the witch's crown.

Mrs. Raudabusch shook her head and went back to her desk. Big girls wanted to check out books. She had to rubber-stamp the cards. I would stay in Narnian time.

Imagine! All over the place, around the corner, new worlds— places where I could hide and never be found. I read on, biting my fingernails as the lion whom I had believed was going to save the day got tied to the stone table by hags, ogres, incubuses, wolves. Then stabbed to death by the White Witch! I chewed the inside of my cheek. I didn't get it. He'd had a nice walk that evening through the forest with the two girls who adored him—I really thought he was going to get away, but he actually volunteered himself to his murderers. Let them tie him up—didn't resist. What was he thinking? Before the bad guys kill Aslan, they call him names and cut off his mane. Next thing you know, the stone table cracks, his body disappears, but, wow, what a neat idea, an all-new Aslan with a freshly regrown mane bounds in, trouncing the witch and all her evil companions.

Sound familiar? Not to me. I thought this story the most original I had ever read. I went through the whole thing without recognizing Aslan as a Christ figure, never suspecting that he had undergone a crucifixion, having no clue what crucifixion was. I hadn't encountered the term.

A year later, out for a walk on a snowy Christmas morning, I felt astonished to run into friends carrying schoolbags.

"You're not going to school?"

"We are!"

I was bewildered. Didn't Batya and Devorah like presents? "But it's Christmas!" I said in disbelief.

"We go to school on Christmas!" they said angrily, and someone explained to me that they were Jewish—different from Christian—that Christianity and Judaism were *religions*. Never having associated Christmas with religion, I didn't get the point.

We were short on Bibles at our house, but we still had religion. Instead of a cross or a mezuzah, we had a living room shelf crammed with thumbed-through Theodor Reik tomes, next to our unread set of the Harvard Classics. After Mom and Dad fought, I'd see their tense faces seeking an uplifting passage in one of their autographed copies, Reik's *Masochism in Modern Man*, perhaps, or *Psychology of Sex Relations*. My mother so prided herself on these books, which had been there since before I was born, that she grew angry when I accidentally dislodged one. For a long time, I didn't know who this Reik guy was, but I knew that my parents bowed down to him. I thought we got those books from our friend, "Aunt" Berkeley, of the tight smile, iron-gray bun, sensible shoes, and string of pearls. The light shone in Dad's eyes when he talked about her. I could almost hear a heavenly choir.

My father's psychoanalyst, Dr. Ruth P. Berkeley, worshiped Theodor Reik, her own psychoanalyst, contributing to a *Festschrift* for him in 1953 and writing gushing reviews of his books. Born poor on an isolated farm in a remote redneck hamlet, Dr. Berkeley could claim a pure gold analytic pedigree reaching back to Sigmund Freud, who analyzed Karl Abraham, who analyzed Theodor Reik. Hickory-nut pioneer all over her homespun face, Ruth Berkeley could trade in her yahoo Bible Belt identity for that of Freudian sophisticate, converting to the local religion, psychoanalysis.

"Aunt" Berkeley, as my brother and I were told to call her, made visitations. Wearing her jovial smile and silk print dresses, she appeared on Thanksgiving, on Easter, and at assorted birthdays and dinners. Dad went to her house by himself. A lot.

Sometimes Mom went, too, all dressed up and looking tense, but the two of them never visited her as a couple.

Whenever "Aunt" Berkeley was expected at our place, my parents hovered near the front door, toddlers on their best behavior, eager for Mommy's attention. The doorbell rang, and scuffles ensued: who would get to let her in? Once, Mom—getting to the door first—yanked it open, squealing, "*Dr.* Berkeley! Hello!"

As the plump figure stood blinking under our bright hall lights, Dad stepped past Mom and hugged her. Aunt Berkeley smiled, an overweight Madonna adoring her apostles and saints. I couldn't help but notice Dad's cheeks glowing, his chest expanding, at the sight of his heroine, who haunts our family albums, her image lurking in places where I don't even remember seeing her—collecting a lily in the middle of a moor with her botanist daughter on one of our family vacations on Nantucket. Smack-dab in the middle of a wide white picnic blanket showcasing her baking and cooking talents, spread in the backyard of her weekend home in Valley Forge. Dinner tables. At her house. At our house. At a Chinese restaurant. In some photos, I'm a babe in arms—her arms, or those of her pretty teenage daughter. I couldn't help but notice the way Dr. Berkeley beamed at Dad—encouragingly, lovingly, approvingly. She sent Mom downcast glances, as if wondering whether Dad had gotten a good deal.

"My, this tastes wonderful!" Dad sighed, tucking into Virginia ham, one of Aunt Berkeley's specialties. Dad, Mom, my brother, and I were seated around Aunt Berkeley's big round table.

Porcelain knickknacks and dusty sofas covered with afghans filled the room. This was Aunt Berkeley's parlor, and she loved to bustle into it with platters of ham, roasted turkey, and gravy.

"That's *my* redeye gravy!" she said, as Mom's face fell. A steaming tureen of grits—Dad's other favorite food, and not one Mom knew how to cook—appeared, swimming with butter.

I took hold of that huge white china tureen when Aunt Berkeley handed it to me and passed it to my brother Roland. One look at Mom's face and I didn't want to give her a chance to accidentally up-end those creamy grits.

Roland ladled himself some grits and put the dish on the side of his plate furthest from Mom.

The look of ecstasy on Dad's face as he smelled his buttery grits and his fork wormed its way through Aunt Berkeley's delicacies told me not to interrupt. Cooking was never Mom's forte—she mixed food the way she mixed paints, for texture and color—and while Dad and Aunt Berkeley oohed and ahhed over the ham, Mom looked as though she wanted to dive under the table mat.

"I make it with Coca-Cola," Aunt Berkeley announced, hurrying in with yet another dish, biscuits, probably, in her pot holder-clad hands, an apron covering her dress. Mom's face twitched. She bought Coke for Macie, our cleaning lady and cook, but we children were not allowed to drink it.

"Well, now, we don't hold with folks who make it with coffee, do we?" Dad nodded, looking up at Aunt Berkeley, perpetual adoration in every line of his face, a napkin tucked under his chin.

"No, we don't," Aunt Berkeley said, patting his shoulder before turning politely, almost as an afterthought, toward my mother. "Won't *you* have some, Celine?" A slightly wounded tone infused her words. Mom's tight-lipped expression did not voice enthusiasm for the spread.

"Oh, just a teeny bit! No, no, not more! *Just* a spoonful!" Mom said, with a wide smile and arched eyebrows, waving away the meal as if it were a bad smell. Patting her slender waist, Mom declared, "Have to watch my weight!" her eyes narrowing at the flabby outlines of both Aunt Berkeley and Dad. A platter of green beans, at which Mom wrinkled her nose, went around the table.

"Did you know cooking vegetables too long destroys vitamins?" she asked. Neither Dad nor Aunt Berkeley answered. Dad was smiling as the doctor leaned over him, tucking "just a little more" biscuits and gravy onto his heavily laden plate.

"I'm happy as a pig in shit," Dad said, mouth full, gazing at Aunt Berkeley, who blushed.

I fiddled with my fork and peeped at Mom, who was looking in the opposite direction as though determined not to notice Dad or Aunt Berkeley.

Once we'd cleaned our plates, Dr. Berkeley cleared the table and brought in dessert, a big layer cake. She cut us all slices, except for Mom, who shook her head. Aunt Berkeley fussed over Dad, making sure he had had enough.

"I'm watching my weight!" Mom said, fending off the cake as Aunt Berkeley approached her again.

As we ate, I felt Mom's eyes on my plate. She leaned toward me, eyes filled with longing. "Could I have just a teeny-*weensy* bit?" she asked, plunging her fork into my cake and closing her eyes in a display of pleasure so exaggerated I felt embarrassed. I pushed my plate away.

Back in 1940, when Dad was single, he had been Dr. Berkeley's very first patient. Like her, he appreciated deep-dish raspberry pies, knew how to mix biscuit dough and bake it. A homely, menopausal fifty-three to Dad's handsome thirty-something, Dr. Berkeley, like him, could not go home again—and like him, she was homesick.

The two had in common their sense of exile, lovers of Manhattan fated to be oddballs by virtue of their highly noticeable accents. Dad, with his prissy ways and his inability to chat or joke without a stiff drink and a cigarette, Dr. Berkeley, her thin, leathery lips looking pursed even when smiling, could share merry, but not sexual, moments. Somehow, it was revealed that Dad's prophet was getting a divorce. The implosion of Dr. Berkeley's marriage had dovetailed with the U.S. Army's rejection of my father.

"Marry me!" he said.

"You know I can't do that. Lie back down on the couch and say what comes to mind."

When I look at photos of Dad from the time he first entered analysis with Dr. Berkeley, I deduce that he must have been a temptation. A dashing young blade in a white suit, those long-fingered hands of his poised elegantly over the keyboard or casually lighting a cigarette, he must have looked like the kind of guy she could never get. Like many a patient, he fell in love with the messiah. Like many a high priestess, she didn't grant his wish.

Instead of her body and blood, she handed him containers of little red Seconals and big yellow Nembutals, which took pride of place on his dresser the entire time I was growing up. I can still remember the pop of those plastic lids, the click of the containers

being set back on the wooden dresser. Dad gulped his pills with gin and tonics before settling down to sleep, a nightcap pulled over his head, a transistor radio singing under his ear.

"She had the most beautiful eyes," Dad would tell me many years later, after the doctor finally died in her mid-nineties. He sighed with longing.

"Well, now, let's fold our napkins," Aunt Berkeley said, rising from the table. She smiled at Dad, who was eyeing his glass.

"We've got some very fine apple cider for the children, and some other drinks for the grown-ups," she said. Dad moved toward the cocktail cart; Aunt Berkeley hurried after, making sure he knew where to find the bitters. Mom hung back in the doorway, looking as though she'd prefer a glass of orange juice.

There was something about the way Aunt Berkeley and Dad looked at each other, sometimes commiserating, sometimes with eyes twinkling in a private joke, that made me feel sorry for Mom.

FOUR

The Intervention

It falles me here to write of Chastity,
That fairest vertue, farre aboue the rest

EDMUND SPENSER, *The Faerie Queen*

Sherry's acne, protruding like smallpox pustules, was one of the things I was going to miss about summer camp. Closing the cabin door behind her, she headed down the hill. The other girls peeked through the shutters to see whether she was out of earshot.

Ellen spoke first, turning with a grin as soon as Sherry was on the path through the pines.

"There she goes," Ellen cocked an eyebrow, insinuation in every syllable, "the girl who keeps Noxzema in business." Ellen was the one who dyed the cafeteria milk green, smeared BENGAY on the boys' toilet seats, and made animal noises after lights out.

Ellen never got into trouble. She had mastered the art of looking innocent when culpable. Although I was always innocent, because I was too scared to break a single rule, I usually *felt* guilty, so the counselors suspected me of misdemeanors that took place only in my dreams. I loved Ellen's wild ways and admired her guts. She seemed happy all the time.

"And her face still looks like a dartboard," Ellen added. Weak giggles. We'd heard the dartboard joke all summer. We wanted some new Sherry joke, since it was the end of the season.

"So what could Sherry do with her face?" Ellen asked.

"Hide it!" I said, since that was what I liked to do with my own. Seven other thirteen-year-old girls choked and farted with laughter. I was so surprised that I jumped, almost tumbling out of my bunk.

"That's what I'll miss," Ellen gasped, when she finally caught her breath. She didn't mean my startle reflex.

But I started to cry.

Before I knew it, she'd put her arm around me. I froze with embarrassment; sympathy made me cry, and I was afraid to think of Ellen as a friend. I pulled back, and she eyed me cautiously.

"You should maybe see the camp psychologist."

"The who?"

"I was sad and she helped."

"You?"

"When I got my first period, my mother slapped me."

"Why would she do that?"

Ellen's face twisted, and I wished I'd kept my mouth shut. After a moment, she said, "The psychologist talked to her, and my mom and I get along now. Sort of."

Right after dinner, I followed directions through the pines down to the small house by the lake. A blonde, roly-poly lady in a tie-dye muumuu opened the door, setting the wind chimes on her porch tinkling.

"Well, hello there!" she chirped, and I stiffened. "Come right in."

A veritable jungle of spider plants hung from her windows; yucca and cactus lined the walls. Pine-scented candles burned in corners around the room, failing to mask the odor of pot and cigarettes.

She waved me toward a large, comfy armchair and started opening windows as I eased into it. Swish, swish, went the muumuu, and she sat across from me.

"How about some tea?" She reached for a dusty pottery bowl wavy with some camper's best efforts and filled to the brim with mint tea bags. I hoped it wasn't mixed with pot. She was already setting a battered kettle on a hot plate.

"I don't like tea," I said.

I remembered drinking coffee with my father every morning—hot milk, sugary coffee, and baking-powder biscuits.

"Let's hear your story. Just what brought you here."

"A mistake. It's nothing—I was crying and a girl in my bunk thought I should come. I'm really fine now."

"OK. Is there any activity you especially liked at camp?"

That was easy. "Well, I enjoyed the modern dance classes. The teacher said I was good."

I rose from the armchair, which had felt too soft anyway.

"Of course," she said, her voice so soft it was almost a whisper. "I understand." But, she asked, would I mind telling her why I'd felt sad *before*? I burst into tears yet again. I don't remember what I told her, but images flashed through my mind of my red-faced, disheveled father exhaling gin, a shock of hair falling over his forehead, grabbing me, slapping me, my mother, eyes wide, running out of the room, my brother reeking of pot and sweat. The thought of going home made me want to dig a hole and hide. I talked in a frenzy, stopping when I noticed the sky darkening from golden to pale orange as early evening moved toward night.

I was in the oldest group and so could not return to camp, unless I wanted to train as a counselor the following summer. But I hated the thought of telling other campers what to do; I wanted to get lost in the group, sticking gobs of papier-mâché onto a mask, not tell other kids how to do that. I'd been running to summer camps since I was ten. Eight solid weeks away from home. A godsend.

Except for visiting day. On the least disastrous of these, my mother swam from her bed-and-breakfast across the cove to the camp, hauling herself up unexpectedly on a grassy lakefront area near the tennis courts while practically the whole camp was there: we were all heading toward the dining hall for lunch.

"Who's that lady? She's waving at you. Do you know her? Is that your, your—?" The girls giggled, bug-eyed with horror or amusement, as Mom, in a suit that looked like a white ballerina tutu, waved and made an extravagant curtsy.

"Oh, just some monkey." I hoped to pass her off as a wandering lunatic, unrelated to me, but when she called my name loudly, adding "It's Mom!" as though I'd accidentally failed to recognize her, I had to wave back, or watch her make friends with anyone willing to talk to her. She sang louder, clapped harder, expressed everything more than anyone else. At least Dad wasn't with her. My brother was back at the B&B sleeping off whatever drug he'd tried the night before.

"Your whole family should go into therapy together," the muumuu lady breathed. "You need family therapy." She never said exactly what family therapy was, but the way she waved her arms around while her eyes misted over made me think it worked like magic.

I imagined my family sitting around this room, Dad grinding his jaw and jigging his knee, Mom grinning angrily, Roland chatting with persons whom neither I nor anyone else could see or hear. I remembered Dad throwing the radio and how it smashed into pieces against the wall after I'd ducked. What would he throw when I told him the camp psychologist said we should all go to family therapy? She said she was willing to talk with my father alone or with my family, "whenever you feel ready." I wanted to jump up and announce that I'd been *feeling* ready for the past thirteen years, all my life, where have you been, and do you provide shields or armor? As she talked, I could almost hear her muumuu dragging across the floor while she herded Dad, Mom, and Roland into those overstuffed armchairs. I sat back and watched. Dad agreed to abandon drinking and violence. Mom announced that she'd learn to be a mother. Roland's eyes came into focus as he expressed regret for getting stoned: he'd like to finish high school after all. The whole thing took maybe twenty minutes, and we were done.

I told the lady everything I could think of about my family, not mentioning that if I looked at a mirror, a girl so hideous that passersby flinched at the sight of her stared back. But even so, I was gloating: after family therapy, my problems wouldn't hold a candle to the scrapes that characters in *The Brady Bunch* endured. Plus, I'd have smooth-as-silk skin that never needed Noxzema.

"We should go into family therapy," I told my mother when she came to pick me up. "The camp psychologist told me that." Mom placed her hands on her hips, raised her eyebrows exaggeratedly, and stared.

"You know, I almost didn't recognize you! You're, well, taller," she lied, staring with disapproval at my newly sprouted breasts.

I'd put on ten pounds, too, mostly on my newly widened hips. At this camp, you could buy candy whenever you wanted, instead of only once a week, like at my old camp.

I dropped the family therapy subject but raised it later, while Dad was watching TV and I was cleaning the guinea pigs' cage.

Dad started shaking me. My head snapped back and forth, and I thought about dying before we got to try family therapy.

He'd been grabbing my hand anytime we left the house together. I hated it.

"When are you going to get a family therapist?" I asked my mother the next day.

"I'm looking into possibilities," she said, averting her eyes. "But family therapy is hardly necessary," she informed me.

Had I known that Daddy goes three days a week to Aunt Berkeley, the psychoanalyst? And that works just fine, she said, in her low voice, without looking me in the eye, as if she were afraid he would hear her—and he might. She herself went to Aunt Berkeley occasionally, she said, and it was time I had a psychoanalyst of my own. The way she talked, I thought of going to the psychoanalyst as something you just do, as an embarrassing and unexpected consequence of growing up, the way you get your period. I remembered telling Mom that I'd finally gotten mine, and how she'd seemed not to know which way to look. A year earlier, I'd taken her aside and begged for a trainer bra, because girls at school were laughing at me for wearing an undershirt. Mom made a point of telling Dad that we were going to buy school shoes, "and maybe a bra!" as if a more ridiculous request could not be imagined. At the local department store, a harassed saleslady could find no bra small enough to fit my rib cage. I stood in the unflattering light of the changing room with that thing flopping down to my navel as my mother smirked. ("Serves you right! You don't need one!") The saleslady shook her head sympathetically, saying, "You got to let your puppies grow."

My mother said she would talk to Aunt Berkeley and interview psychoanalysts. When they found a good one, they would let me know. I was still disappointed about family therapy, but it was beginning to dawn on me that I'd get to see this analyst after school. That would shave off a few of the hours I would otherwise have to spend with my family.

When Dr. Berkeley made her recommendation, I asked no questions. Mom handed me a phone number and urged me to call and make my own appointment. Dr. Oscar Sternbach, a Viennese refugee from Hitler, as he was to tell me, wasn't a doctor, but I didn't find that out until later.

FIVE

In the Beginning

Each time we have a quarrel
It almost breaks my heart . . .

DOC POMUS AND MORT SHUMAN, "Teenager in Love"

I can still see myself on my way to my first appointment: a pale teenager with messy, dark blonde hair in a purple tie-dye T-shirt, blue jeans, and blue clogs. A schoolbag over my shoulder, I was walking away from a crowd of classmates, who called after my retreating back, asking where I was going, since normally we walked together to the bus stop. Too embarrassed to reply, I yelled, while edging, then running, toward the other bus stop, "I have an appointment!" I felt sure I was the only girl in my class, probably in the whole school, who was seeing a psychoanalyst. Even so, this secret was the one thing I had to call my own.

Entering the psychoanalyst's building, I glanced at the doorman, imagining myself to be so ugly that he could hardly bear to glance at me. I lived in a state of fear. I was always wishing someone would help me decide what to do or supply me with the courage I needed. I spent most of my time alone in my room making candles or playing with my guinea pigs. Occasionally I walked to the health food store on 106th Street, where I bought a tiger's milk bar to eat on the way to the bookstore on 114th. There, I bought books with titles like *White Racism: A Psychohistory* but found myself unable to get past the first paragraph. What I really wanted was not this scholarly tome whose argument remained over my head but rather some explanation of my father, whom I thought of as a racist slave driver just because he grew up white in segregated North Carolina and spoke with a strong southern accent. I associated his accent with the Ku Klux Klan. Actually, he was no racist; I just felt like a slave around him. The book offered no explanation of Dad, failing to tackle my sense of him as Simon Legree, myself as his most interesting victim. I often went into the bathroom to study my ugliness in the mirror. My shoulders looked deformed. One eye seemed higher than the other. One breast looked smaller than the other. So ugly. People who saw me on the street probably winced.

I was fourteen the first time I went to Sternbach's office. After I was buzzed in via intercom, I found myself in a foyer dominated by warlike terra-cotta Roman statues and a huge dark-wood desk. A full-length mirror in a gold-edged Venetian frame hidden behind the front door took me by surprise. One unexpected glimpse, and I felt shabby in my Levi's and T-shirt.

George Grosz etchings peopled by criminals and abject drinkers, dark oil paintings, and French caricatures dominated Sternbach's walls. A cast-iron gate, elaborately carved, led into a room crammed with Biedermeier furniture arranged on Persian carpets, walls hung with paintings of the Alps in ornate golden frames, and then the one thing we had at home as well: a grand piano. My father kept two pianos in his music room. No one played the third, in our living room. I had never seen rooms like Sternbach's anywhere outside of museums and almost had the feeling that I had gone back in time to some much earlier era—I hoped a better one.

A man with salt-and-pepper hair emerged from a dark hallway into the foyer in which I stood. He shook my hand and looked me over with an air of concern.

"I am Dr. Sternbach," he said. With a courtly wave of his hand, he motioned me down the dark hallway. I was far more inclined

to go through the white French doors in the waiting room, since the aroma of some spicy goulash issued from what was clearly the kitchen behind. The whole foyer smelled of warmth and good food. But I followed him. Opening a door, he motioned me toward a comfortable side chair, and I sank into it. I felt frightened without knowing why.

The furniture, the objets d'art, seemed an insignificant backdrop to the man himself. An elderly—so it seemed to me at fourteen—gentleman, his dignified accent impressed me. I was used to school friends remarking that my southern father "talked funny," and here was a different, better accent. Dr. Sternbach looked to be in his early sixties. He was portly, had a face I thought kind, with gold-rimmed glasses perched on his nose, and wore a silk tie.

"Why are you here?"

This room, like his foyer, was so distracting I could hardly answer his question. But if I'd dared to say what I felt, I would have told him that I liked his house better than mine, that it was quiet here, restfully quiet. No one was yelling. The aromas of the place were fabulous, something that smelled like big old hunks of meat incubating—unidentifiable spices wafting from his kitchen, differing from my father's southern cooking, but delicious. Staring at the art on Dr. Sternbach's walls helped me forget I'd have to leave and go back to my house in another forty-odd minutes.

I looked at him, and what came out of my mouth was, "Where did you get those weird masks?"

"We are not talking about me, but about you," he said quietly.

"I hate myself," I remarked, and immediately wanted to forget what I'd just said. I began to daydream. I could almost hypnotize myself with the thought of certain favorite scenes. I thought with love of the brown water tanks on top of the buildings, the way the sun set over the trees in Riverside Park. Dr. Sternbach sat, waiting.

"I can't concentrate in school."

He nodded.

I went for broke. "And I hate my father."

He sat up straight, and I felt that I'd woken him up. A small shiver of pleasure went through me. If I could shock him, this could be fun, or at least I'd feel better than when I came in.

"You hate your father? Can you tell me why, please?"

Suddenly I felt that I was going to cry, because I did love my father, who had, earlier that week, screamed "Get the hell out!" when I entered his music room wearing glasses that had new, round, tortoiseshell frames, too different for him from the pale blue ones with glitter that I'd worn since third grade. But I didn't mention the incident.

"Your mother says that you want to run away from home."

My mother only knew what she'd read in my journal. And then I did cry, because I wanted to have the strength to pack my bags, ask directions from strangers, get a job, find a boarding school or a place to live. I felt ashamed not to be doing anything to save myself. I wanted to tell Dr. Sternbach the most embarrassing thing: that I was afraid people on the street would be harmed by seeing how ugly I was. But he interrupted my thoughts. I wanted to wait a moment and try to explain.

He leaned forward, hands on his knees. "Please try to tell me why you are here, what you would like to get out of treatment."

That was a question I could answer.

"I want to be free. I hate my school, and I'm no good at math or biology, but they say you have to take it anyway. I want to go to a free school where the students decide what they want to study. And I know there's one in upstate New York and I want to go there. Have you read *Summerhill: A Radical Approach to Childrearing*?"

I thought I saw him start to smile, so I did not dare explain how much I admired Summerhill's headmaster, A. S. Neill. I was afraid Dr. Sternbach would not like him.

I had corresponded with Neill several times, asking to be admitted and for help in dealing with my parents. "Dear Melissa," he had written, "But I can't help you with your troubles. How could I? What advice could I give you? I don't know you, don't know what sort of a kid you are, honest, dishonest, bad tempered, bitchy. See what I mean. You'll have to try to find your own happiness without advice from me or anyone else. Not very helpful, am I?"

"Do they have therapy at this free school? Because I think you would need it," Dr. Sternbach said, with a concerned look. He leaned back in his La-Z-Boy, his hands folded over his paunch.

He spoke with great authority.

"Could you please tell me about who you are, what made you become a psychoanalyst?" I asked.

"I am a master," he informed me. "You know, *I* was analyzed by Paul Federn."

My embarrassment at not knowing the name must have conveyed itself, for Dr. Sternbach immediately pointed to his crammed bookshelf. There, in a place of honor, surrounded by small oval family photographs arranged so as to resemble admiring worshippers, sat a bronze bust of Federn, of the bald head and pained expression.

"Now *he* was loyal to Freud!" Sternbach told me, waving a forefinger. So loyal, I learned, that Federn became known as the Apostle Paul. Like Theodor Reik, and like Sternbach's other psychoanalyst, Ludwig Jekels, another name that my analyst seemed grieved to find I had not heard, Federn was among the Viennese inner circle of Sigmund Freud himself. Oscar Sternbach could trace his lineage back to God, his sainthood to his

Jewish refugee status. Ultimately, Sternbach encouraged me to purchase a *Standard Edition of the Complete Psychological Works of Sigmund Freud* and to read and study it, which I did, underlining passages and inking in marginal comments.

When Dr. Sternbach asserted that Federn and Jekels "were much closer to Freud" than Reik—whose name provoked a sniff—I understood that my analyst was so high in the pantheon that he could look down at the balding heads of these archangels. Reik's book, *Listening with the Third Ear,* was old stuff. But Dr. Sternbach had a Theodor Reik story up his sleeve for one of my first sessions.

"My wife and I invited Dr. Reik for dinner," he declaimed, "and our daughter, she was seven years old," he added. "She stared at Reik all through dinner before asking him where his third ear was!" He laughed loudly.

I was in the presence of a high priest, if not a magician, surrounded by Dr. Sternbach's gold-limned books and Egyptian figurines, his couch enshrined in a bright red cloth, Aztec designs snaking through it. He told a story of a woman patient complaining, when she ran into him outside on a wintry day, "God doesn't wear an overcoat." Idols abounded: huge mahogany African masks boasting gigantic, phallic noses and large-lipped mouths practically jumped off the walls. A somber portrait of Freud, cigar in hand, hung on the wall above Sternbach's phone. Dr. Sternbach's office, with its storm windows fifteen flights up and the low hum of that white noise machine in the waiting room, seemed quiet as a shrine. Between the silence and the exotic art, I thought of it as a vast improvement over home, what with daily screaming matches between my parents. I felt a certain unquestioning loyalty, worshiping his décor.

I walked home in a dream from my very first session. A wise old man who knew everything wanted to listen to me. I couldn't have hoped for better.

When I returned for my next session, he pointed to some mittens I had left in my chair.

"You see, that means you want to return for analysis to me," he said, smiling. "You forgot them because you would like to come here again," he said in such a sweet, avuncular way that

I loved him. I agreed. I enjoyed the peaceful quiet of the room. For the first time in my life, I wasn't listening for a scream or a yell from one of my parents, or waiting to hear a blow fall.

Psychoanalysis offered hours away from Mom, Dad, Roland, who was smoking hash, dropping acid, never taking a bath, playing drums at all hours. Even the brief deliverance offered by the forty-five-minute therapy hour plus the extra fifteen-minute ride to my analyst's office and back again made it all worthwhile. Summer camp and school had offered one escape; psychoanalysis offered another.

True, I wanted to escape more than my home: I wanted escape from a compulsion to talk about sex, especially forms of it as bizarre as my imagination could conjure at that age, mostly involving vampires. I couldn't figure out why everyone else wasn't as interested in talking about sex and got weird looks when I mentioned the subject yet again. I'd been reading Wilhelm Reich, who claimed that orgasms were the key to salvation, and I felt fairly sure that I had to be doing something with a boy to experience what I dimly knew must be the greatest of pleasures. Therefore, I wanted to meet a boy, and maybe Dr. Sternbach could tell me how to do that. Desperation, or loneliness, occasionally drove me to confide in one parent or my brother, and I always regretted doing so. I often retreated to my room to cuddle my guinea pigs, with the embarrassed realization that I might as well talk to them. There were the paralyzing depressions, the days when I could hardly force myself out of the house but, when I did, could not bear to speak to anyone.

In my first sessions, I sat in a chair, having been told that the couch was for later—I assumed when I was a big girl. I fretted. Did he find me too immature for the real thing?

"Have you ever had an orgasm?" Sternbach asked. He leaned back in his La-Z-Boy and eyed me.

I sat up in my considerably less comfortable chair—even then I found it unfair that he got the nice chair—and informed him, with great primness, "I've never yet met a boy with whom I would like to have an orgasm."

His laugh, of scorn or amazement, or both, filled the room. I sat uneasily, knowing I'd said something stupid.

"You don't have to be with a boy," he gasped for air, "to have an orgasm!" He chuckled. "Do you rub your clitoris? Yes?"

No, I didn't. I had expected to snare Sternbach with my extensive knowledge of sexuality and boys, so the conversation was not going well. I thought I knew more than some girls. I wasn't the idiot who thought she was dying of cancer when she got her first period. I'd known about menstruation since fourth grade. Discovering a health form from a summer camp on the floor of the school bus, I asked the bus driver the meaning of a word— *men-you-stration*? He reddened and wouldn't explain.

"Why won't you tell me?" I demanded of the driver.

"You gotta ask your mother," he insisted.

Aghast—*how could you ask the bus driver?*—Mom said she'd tell me on the condition that I never mention the subject to my brother. Her face distraught, she spoke at length, but all I could remember was that bleeding had something to do with pregnancy, and that the subject would somehow endanger my brother, or at least scare him as much as it scared her. At the dinner table, bristling with suppressed curiosity and nerves, I asked my brother whether he'd ever heard of *menyoustration*. He hadn't, and wasn't interested, but Mom's face registered indignation.

In sixth-grade health class, I sailed through the Disney *Story of Menstruation* movie with the feeling that I already knew that stuff. The class laughed when Miss Kidder, cheeks flushing at the sight of the wooden female body from which she was forced to teach the facts of life, unscrewed, with a tormented expression, two things on top. Raising each round thing high, as if making two Nazi salutes, looking to the side as though she couldn't bear to see the contents of her hands, she announced, "These are the breasts."

I sighed. I almost wanted to borrow those big ones displayed by Miss Kidder. We squirmed in our trainer bras.

Around Sternbach, I felt as dumb as Miss Crissey, the elderly biology teacher who had seen a drawing of a condom on the board and asked, "What's that?" My classmates and I had snickered at her failure to recognize the contraceptive that we were determined to use when the opportunity presented itself. Secretly, I wondered how condoms worked. I was afraid to ask how you got that floppy thing, the penis, into the loose, rubbery tube that looked like the finger hole in a glove. Only when I slow-danced for the first time with a boy at the ninth-grade dance—four bars into "A Whiter Shade of Pale," and a few months after I'd met Sternbach—did the answer press itself against my thigh.

Each time I arrived for a session, I hoped to feel that Dr. Sternbach found me intelligent, observant—that he would admire what I was reading or thinking. Sometimes he called me "little rat." He said that was a German term of endearment.

I found that any mention of my interest in boys or what I regarded as sophisticated experimentation amused or irritated him rather than increasing his regard. But I hardly knew what else to tell him. When I announced that a boy at the school dance had snuck me out of the school auditorium and into the stairwell, where we kissed in total darkness, I expected Sternbach to say I was bad, or daring. Instead, he laughed.

"But it was French kissing!" I protested.

He laughed again. "The difference between French kissing and sex is the difference between fine, thick whipped cream, the kind you have in Vienna on top of a Sacher torte, and that horrible white powder Americans put in their coffee."

"Coffee-mate?" I asked.

"*You* know—I don't," he said.

I felt my ever-diminishing range of knowledge shrink with each disdainful look from Sternbach.

I liked to make fudge. I used my father's cookbook, the one his mother had given him, *The Settlement Cookbook* (subtitled *The Way to a Man's Heart*).

Sternbach looked me over. He wondered whether I'd like to make him some fudge.

I had a cooking thermometer, and I described, at length, the process of making fudge, the necessity of dropping a dollop of the mix into cold water until a ball formed—the soft-ball phase. At my mention of the soft-ball stage, his eyes widened and he snickered, shifting in his seat. He tapped on his belt buckle and crossed his legs.

"So do you like the *fucking* fudge?"

Startled, I answered that yes, I had liked the fudge that I had made.

Around this time, he asked me to find and sew on a button for his gray wool cardigan. He held his sweater up for me, one he often wore, asking whether I thought I could manage that. I folded it and took it home, carefully selected a button from my sewing box and sewed it on. I brought the sweater back to the next session, expecting to be praised for my quick but thoughtful work. Instead, he complained. The button I'd chosen wasn't right for the sweater—*no button I could have chosen would have been right*—therefore, he said, I was resisting him and, by doing so, resisting analysis.

"Look at this!" he said, holding the sweater up. "Did you not even look at the buttonholes before you sewed on this button?" He shook his head in disgust.

By the end of my session, I realized that I was inconsiderate and careless, and felt sad. I had failed him, and he was only trying to help me.

"Well, maybe I should not exploit your masochism," he murmured.

He talked often about my masochism, remarking that my mother was a masochist. I was unclear on the definition of what would become his favorite topic in our many years together. So he gave me an example: *a woman patient had dreamed of sucking off a regiment of soldiers.*

Although I was already fourteen, I hadn't heard the term "sucking off," and had yet to desire the act, but after Sternbach's detailed description of the woman's dream, I figured out what he meant. I was wondering why anyone would do that and also curious what this activity had to do with masochism, a term that no definition, no matter how explicit, could have clarified for me at that age. I had just gotten my period and enjoyed thinking about kissing, even though experience so far had not measured up to my daydreams. Other forms of sexual expression had not yet entered my consciousness. I thought it must hurt to

41

kneel down on a hard surface like a road while engaging in an activity so strenuous as sucking on a penis. I wondered what you held on to while you moved your mouth—the knees? The thighs? I remained somewhat unclear on the matter of erections, had never seen a boy ejaculate, did not know how long the sucking was supposed to go on, and did not realize that oral sex was something people desired. Knowing I'd missed something, I asked, "What's masochistic about sucking off a regiment of soldiers?"

Yet again, laughter burst from him—he was holding his sides. I thought I'd pleased him but wasn't sure.

"I think I said something boring," I mused.

"On the contrary, I find you most amusing."

He was still chuckling as I left his office to go home, feeling that, finally, I had done something right.

SIX

Two to Tango

> With what price we pay
> for the glory of motherhood.
>
> ISADORA DUNCAN

I sat in the dark movie theater forgetting my popcorn, thrilled to see Isadora Duncan rush breathlessly up to the Elgin marbles. Cut to shots of her dancing through a sun-drenched Parthenon in a sun-drenched toga. With that wide-eyed enthusiasm—the way she clasped her hands to her chest and promised to invigorate Western art—she reminded me of Mom, who was sitting beside me, not enjoying the show. I liked best the part that *didn't* remind me of Mom, the part forcing an annoyed titter from her, the part where Isadora learns enough Russian to tell her Slavic lover, "Darling, you have *beautiful* thighs." After that steamy episode, Isadora, back onstage in Boston, dancing for a black-tie crowd, undoes the top of her toga, swinging her bare breasts around. The orchestra plays on, eyes riveted on the topless wonder, while the audience gasps and cries, "Whore!"

Isadora retorts, "My body is *free*! My body is *beautiful*!" and dances on until policemen arrive to drag her offstage. Wow. I wanted to feel exactly what she felt—that my body was gorgeous, my breasts, too, that I could dance freedom and dance strength and be loved.

Mom coughed and fidgeted.

Why, I wondered, had Mom taken me to a movie called *Isadora* if she didn't want me to see it?

Mom had thought there would be more *dancing,* she said on the subway home. Isadora was really a great *dancer*—no need to sensationalize the sordid aspects of her life the way that actress Vanessa Redgrave did. Dance was a great art, Mom said, and she had enjoyed ballet for years as a teenager, until she developed a habit of eating whole jars of peanut butter and the boys in the pas de deux class couldn't lift her anymore.

"Really?" I said. "*You* were fat?" The subway rattled along— we were somewhere around 72nd Street, and I wondered how much I'd learn before we had to get off at 110th. I was astonished to learn that Mom, like me, had once felt the need to count calories.

"But when you met Dad, you were thin?" I looked sideways at her to see if she would tell me. Photos of Mom, still single at thirty-one, reveal her as a knockout, long brown hair twisted into a coronet, sparkling blue eyes, rosy cheeks, and girlish smile.

"Oh, goodness, yes," Mom said. "I hadn't really noticed I was fat until I was standing there in my tutu and my partner was really huffing and puffing, trying to lift me. Then Mr. Chalif, the teacher, came over and tried. But even he couldn't lift me." That sounded like Mom—not seeing what was right in front of her, even or especially in the mirrored wall of the ballet studio.

"So, you were thin by the time Aunt Berkeley introduced you to Dad?"

Mom nodded. A wistful look crossed her face, as if she knew a fat version of her would not have made the cut. "I'll show you. I have photos of me as a fat fifteen-year-old. I used to lie under a canoe on family beach vacations and read *Oliver Twist* while spooning up big jars of peanut butter."

I looked at tiny, skinny mom—she weighed less than a hundred pounds—and tried to imagine a fat version of her.

"I was quite the buxom teenager," she said. "I'll show you those pictures."

The *Statesville Record and Landmark* had run an engagement photo of my parents, ages thirty-three and forty-two, playing

chopsticks together. Mom was so slim you could see her cheek-bones. But the most noticeable thing about that photograph is that the two of them aren't looking at each other. Dad is smiling at the keyboard. Mom is glancing toward him as her two fingers poke it. If cartoon balloons had been floating over their heads, Mom's would have said, "Aren't I good? Look at me and tell me I'm your best student!" Dad's would have asked, "Do you like my playing? Please reassure me: am I entertaining you?"

Dr. Berkeley had thrown Dad and Mom together two years into Mom's psychoanalysis by inviting most of her patients to a buffet supper party. She seated Mom beside a slim, stiff young man who could barely speak.

Mom remembered him as handsome but pale, almost white, like someone who'd been inside too long, which made me think of Boo Radley. She was quick to add that he got rosier and livened up after he finished one scotch and started sipping another.

Knocking back his third, he drawled, "My, you're sweet!"

Mom hadn't said a word. The skinny fellow clutching the drink was, after all, a man—and he was looking at her. She peeped into his eyes from across the rickety card table at which Dr. Berkeley had seated the two of them.

The loud recorded voice announced, "NEXT STOP 86TH STREET," and Mom jumped, grabbing her tote bag before she realized we still had three more stops to go. "Felicia's jazz dance class helps me watch my figure, you know." She cocked an eyebrow at me. We had had this conversation before, and I could see she hesi-tated to bring up the subject. I didn't reply. "Well, I just thought I'd mention it," Mom said, with a sad look. "I bet you could be good at dance."

She didn't say it, but her eyes did: *Dancers should be thin.*

The train screeched to a stop at 86th Street, and the doors banged open. A voice announced, "Watch da closing doors!" People shuffled on; people shuffled off.

I thought of Isadora and wondered why I'd said no without even trying a class. Because I didn't want to be like Mom? But she seemed nicer, today. She seemed like she wanted to help me. Mom often seemed friendlier when we were not home, where fights erupted, Dad or Roland throwing things.

I wanted to dance like Isadora—wild, free, full of joy. It looked easy—prancing and throwing your arms around to Chopin études.

"Well, OK, I'll try it," I said.

Mom looked surprised, delighted, happy. "You'll need a leotard," she said. "You can borrow one of mine."

The way Mom told it, Aunt Berkeley was a fairy godmother introducing her to Dad. Mom and Dad's wedding album starts with photos of Dr. Berkeley's brownstone labeled "The house where we met." In the center of the page, a smiling photo of "Dr. B." Photos of skinny Mom, grinning from ear to ear, visiting Dad's North Carolina family.

As a reward for her successful analysis—or for getting engaged to Dad—Mom had been invited to join Aunt Berkeley and her daughter Laura on a trip across the American West, and the wedding album is crammed with photos of that journey. Sailing under the Golden Gate Bridge, circumnavigating giant redwoods, Mom longed for her prince. "My thirty-third birthday—a day of black gloom: not a single word from Harry," she wrote under a photo taken in Muir Woods of "Laura and I as tree-trunk elves."

By the time she hit the bottom of the Grand Canyon, Mom seemed to have landed at the end of her patience. "A moment after this picture was taken," she wrote under a picture of herself with the Berkeleys, eating sandwiches by the Colorado River, "I began my two-day journey back to Harry in New York, traveling by ass back, train, police car, bus, and airplane. I reached Idlewild Airport at 10 A.M. on Monday, June 28—Harry's birthday—and Harry was there as I stepped off the plane."

It all sounded so sweet, so romantic, so happy. But happiness doesn't send people to psychiatrists. Grief does. Mom never tired of telling me how, back in 1953, her own mother's unconsummated love for a therapist caused a tailspin. Gaga then consulted "dear Dr. Berkeley." Like Dad, Gaga had hoped for true love with the therapist who penned best sellers with titles like *Help Yourself to Happiness* but skipped town the moment New York State demanded licensing requirements. Besides, Mom confided breathlessly, as a girl of fifteen, Gaga had nearly been sold by her own mother—jealous of the girl's attractiveness—to a man who claimed to be a Russian count. Gaga had begged her mother to allow her to stay, saying she was too young to leave her. The mother gave Gaga a second chance, but only because she hoped to make money by putting Gaga on the stage. Poor Gaga couldn't act and so fell into an unhappy marriage.

Dr. Berkeley distracted Gaga from her lost love with a novel treatment plan: Mom's phone rang.

"Dr. Berkeley calling. Could you please come in for a session to discuss your mother?"

"Of course," said Mom. And so she was ushered into Dr. Berkeley's world.

That Saturday of my first dance class with Felicia, Mom and I strolled into the foyer and saw a huge orange cat sitting in the dance studio. He twitched his tail imperiously until a tall, rail-thin woman with dark hair, about Mom's age, appeared. Bending over on completely straight legs, she scooped up the cat with one hand and told it, "You have to scat, now. It's time for my ladies." She walked past us, pulled open a door, thrust the cat inside, and shut it.

"Oh, hi, Celine," she said. "And this must be Melissa!"

As I came into the studio, I saw it was really an enormous, sunny living room with a red sofa in one corner, a fat gray cat purring on the pillows. Behind me stood shelves lined with books and photos of Felicia's three dancing daughters, who, Mom whispered to me, attended the School of American Ballet. I wanted to look around, take in the room on my own, but Mom pulled me by the elbow to another wall, insisting that I look at a photo of Nureyev and the barre. I knew if I didn't talk to her, she would get louder.

Then she pulled me back to the bookshelf to see another photo of Felicia's eldest daughter in a bullring somewhere, standing high on half-toe with her shoes held way over her head.

"Look at Shana's arms! So graceful!" Mom squealed, grabbing the photo off the shelf and swinging it around like a baton. I wished she'd put that photo down—it wasn't hers! Wouldn't Felicia get mad if Mom kept picking things up?

I turned and found myself facing a full-length mirror. A pale, ugly, chubby girl in a leotard and black tights stared back, and a feeling of hopeless ungainliness came over me. I looked at Felicia, who was sitting on the other side of the room near the record player. She was so graceful.

Her legs were stretching out on either side of her body at what seemed a 180 degree angle, both feet pointed sharply, the upper part of her body down on the floor between her legs. I'd never seen anyone do that, even Isadora. *The Waltz of the Flowers* was playing, and Felicia, in time to the music, slowly raised her arms over her head with her upper body, bending first over one leg, then stretching upright, then leaning over the other side. I was fascinated by her suppleness. I wanted to be able to do what she was doing.

The elevator door banged open again, and women my mother's age poured into the foyer in front of the studio, busily chatting and removing blue jeans, under which they, too, wore black leotards.

Felicia put thick, wooly things on her ankles, carefully pulling the wool up to her knees, and then noticed me watching her. "Have to keep these old muscles toasty. Your Mom says you did some modern dance at summer camp."

"I did take dance," I said, "but we didn't learn how to do that."

Felicia smiled. "Well, let's get you over to the barre. Your mother has wonderful feet, and I'm hoping maybe you do, too." Then she clapped her hands. It occurred to me that I'd been so embarrassed by the sight of Mom doing grand battements on the sidewalk in front of other people that I'd never considered how good her technique was. She was probably strong enough to have been a Rockette. But I also wished I could have seen a photo of plump Mom in a pink tutu with some guy in tights sweating as he tried to lift her. If she could emerge from fatness into ravishing slenderness and be a dancer, then maybe I could, too.

"OK, ladies, let's start. Celine's daughter Melissa is joining us today, and I don't want anyone embarrassing me. Let's see if you can all point your feet properly."

She stood up, leaned over the record player, placed the needle, and then Tina Turner's "Rolling on the River" came on.

Years later, when I was all grown up, I was to make a surprising discovery. Tucked inside our copy of Reik's *Of Love and Lust,* I found a note written by my mother, explaining that on her honeymoon, during their second day at Lake Minnewaska, she and Dad entered the hotel veranda, and "Dr. Reik" was there. Reik, Mom had written, "jumped up and addressed me: 'You—you are not just beautiful—you are delicious!'" My mother added that "of course" she and Dad invited Reik to join them at dinner. Did the honeymooners really sit there with Reik ogling Mom, Dad acting like Reik was doing the two of them an honor? Well, Dad would get even, courting Aunt Berkeley's attentions.

I have often imagined a scene: alcoholic, paranoid Dad moving toward the analytic couch with girlish, frightened Mom, the two of them raising a glass to anything but insight. They had nothing in common but Dr. Berkeley. Throwing together two patients, a virginal thirty-three-year-old with a forty-something penniless piano player—what else could a psychoanalyst do when she couldn't get rid of the urge to sleep with the prince herself?

A wedding photograph of Dr. Berkeley posing between the bride and groom is a theatrical tableau: Dad stares at Mom as if she might run away. Mom clutches Dr. Berkeley's arm. Off in the wings, Theodor Reik awaits his honeymoon cameo appearance.

After about half an hour into Felicia's barre, I was exhausted, but we were nowhere near done. I was sweating. We seemed to be getting a two-minute break. Felicia came over to me, instructing me to point my leg to the side, and I did.

"Now stand up straight—don't lean back!—and hold on to the barre," she commanded, grabbing my foot and lifting my leg up close to my ear. She hesitated somewhere around my elbow.

"Knees straight!" she hissed, and waited to make sure I'd really straightened them.

Then she continued slowly lifting my leg until I felt a tautness in the tendons at the top of my thigh. The stretch felt good, and when I saw my pointed foot soaring into space above my head, I longed for the day when I could hold it there on my own, without Felicia or anyone else helping me.

"Well, that's where *that* is!" Felicia smiled. "You have natural turn-out, too. Let's see those feet." I didn't know what she wanted.

"Why, Melissa! You have terrific extensions!" Mom shrilled, running over. Felicia ignored her and Mom stepped back, folding her arms and wagging her head, as if she wanted to say somebody was being a so-and-so.

"That's *my* daughter!" Mom said, with a big smile.

"Point!" said Felicia, ignoring Mom and looking down at my foot, which I put out to the side. Reminding me to turn out my thigh—"and don't forget, the other thigh, too"—Felicia grabbed my foot, molding it into the correct position. "Look, ladies," she said, including Mom again. "Good feet. Almost as good as your mother's," she said, looking up at me with a smile.

Mom beamed with pride and, one hand on the barre, demonstrated her own fine turn-out.

Not only was Mom not like any of my friends' mothers but she was more like a child than any child I knew. More than once, Mom told me, snickering, that before she met Dad, she had never heard the word *shit*. When Dad used the word at a cocktail party, she stopped him and asked him to define the term. Her eyes got that gleeful look I associated with some new embarrassing thing she might do, like take a bite out of my apple or stick a spoon into my soup instead of her own.

"Well, did you like the class?" Mom asked loudly on the bus going home.

I really had liked the class, liked the music very much, and the idea of being able to do the things Felicia could do. Although the other women were nowhere near as trained, I could see that over months, even going only once or twice a week, they could do things like stand on one leg and move the other one around. They could bend over straight legs and get their hands almost to the floor.

"What are you thinking of?" Mom asked with excessive cheer.

"I wasn't thinking, Mom," I said, as the bus swept through the Central Park transverse. "I'm too tired to think."

"Oh, was the class too much for you?" A look, perhaps of hope, passed over her features.

"No, I'd like to go back."

By the time I saw my mother clearly, decades later, I'd realized my parents had endured a marriage that kept their psychoanalyses going for twenty-five years. Dad drank heavily, opened and slammed shut dresser drawers as he and Mom fought. Mom burst into tears daily. Having children, they both believed, would improve things, so they produced me first and then my brother. Dr. Berkeley encouraged the two of them to tattle on each other in separate sessions, telling Mom that Dad needed his drink, while advising Dad that Mom felt less anxious when she gave people presents.

And throughout my parents' marriage, Dr. Berkeley, matchmaker and savior, remained oblivious to psychological oddities so blatant that I could not help but notice them, even as a distracted teenager. Mom said, one day when I was about fourteen, that she'd believed—"isn't that *ridiculous?*" she asked me—that the word *pedophile* meant "a silly person." She came from a long line of silly persons, but it was to be years before I discovered that. Dr. Berkeley never stumbled over the fact.

When Aunt Berkeley visited us now, I found her formality constraining. Even her laugh seemed artificial. I'd been taken to see her once as a child with my mother, who'd worried about my talking about toilets too much. Aunt Berkeley handed me a bowl of dried apples with milk before intoning, "Well, BM and wee-wee are just things that belong in the toilet, but we don't talk about them at the dinner table."

I remembered eating the apples while thinking about everything Dad and Mom said at the dinner table—maybe they didn't talk about BMs or wee-wee, but they did knock over cups and glare and yell, while Roland and I ducked our heads and ate quickly so we could be excused to our bedrooms, where the sounds of fighting would be muffled. Now I could come to dance class and learn something that would take me away from my parents and their world completely. Dance class was something I had to do with Mom, but at least I had my own spot on the barre.

Felicia had extra tickets, and I got to see the Alvin Ailey company perform *Revelations,* and Judith Jamison perform *Cry.* I was almost in tears, the performances were so beautiful. I wanted to watch Judith Jamison perform *Cry* as often as possible. I wanted to *be* Judith Jamison, so much so that it did not occur to me I was unlikely to grow another five inches and turn into a slim, muscular black woman with incredible technique.

After a few months, Felicia took me aside one day after class and suggested I take ballet classes.

"You're lucky you're so flexible," she said, "and your feet are good. Often, the teen years are quite late to start, but not for someone who might do jazz or modern dance." Felicia had started late herself, I learned, and danced with Alvin Ailey. I could think of nothing I would rather do more.

"But I don't want to do ballet!" I said. "Judith Jamison doesn't do ballet! She does jazz! She does African dance!"

Felicia laughed—a big, enchanting laugh. "Judith Jamison has had *years* of ballet, dear. Years! Judith Jamison goes to ballet class *every day.* Now, there's a wonderful teacher named Maggie Black, but you'd need to go somewhere else for a while—you're a beginner."

I nearly growled. A beginner? I'd been working so hard! For a whole half year, almost!

"Ballet is every dancer's basic training," Felicia explained. "I'll look around and find a teacher who's right for you."

"She's going to need to lose weight," Mom said, sidling up to me. Her eyes were bright. I'd forgotten a bra that day, looked up, saw myself in the mirror, and thought I could maybe look as good as Isadora. I liked having breasts.

"Is this your women's liberation day?" Mom stared pointedly at my breasts, screwed up her eyes, and shook her head. I walked away from the mirror. Felicia suppressed a small sigh.

"Well, yes," Felicia admitted, "there's a little extra weight. But there's time enough for that. I wouldn't worry too much about that right now."

Mom wagged her head.

Well, now I could talk to this Dr. Sternbach about Mom and about what to do about my weight. I hoped. Soon. But the thought of finding my way in ballet and dance made me feel I had something all my own that I loved.

SEVEN

The Group

> All happy families are alike;
> each unhappy family is unhappy in its own way.
>
> LEO TOLSTOY, *Anna Karenina*

One day in the fall of tenth grade, I came home from school, ate two big spoonfuls of honey, and went back to my room. I thought about making myself throw up, but I didn't. I felt extremely ashamed and ugly, and first I just crawled into bed and thought I'd stay there. Or maybe get up and get my leotards together and take the six o'clock jazz dance class at the Alvin Ailey dance center. I often took an afternoon ballet class, then the jazz class. But today I was afraid that if I stayed in bed another second, I wouldn't be able to get up. Ever. Dance felt good, but when I told Dr. Sternbach that, he yelled, "Do you have to feel good all the time? Concentrate on your studies!" Or he talked about opera, and I didn't like opera.

Dad was in his music room with the door shut. Mom was in the kitchen, and I heard banging and clanging. Roland's door was closed, and the smell of pot smoke was heavy in the hall by his room. He had flunked out of two schools in the past two years. I sometimes ran into him in the kitchen, but we didn't talk—gone were the days when we'd gleefully thrown water balloons out his window and read comics together—now I only heard my mother yelling at him when he wrote on the living room wall, and once he threw the can of Ajax at her when she asked him to clean up.

When I went for my next appointment, Dr. Sternbach looked me over and said I seemed depressed. I shrugged. He sat for a while and then said, "Well, it is not surprising. Your family is falling apart."

As he said it, I felt sadder, because up until then, I'd been pushing just that thought out of my mind. There wasn't anything I could do about my brother staying in his room staring blankly, smoking pot, or even, as he had the previous evening, touching the smoldering end of his reefer to a pile of papers on his desk, igniting them, which sent Mom whirling in with a fire extinguisher. There wasn't anything I could do about Dad slamming doors, Mom burning dinner.

"It was never together," I said. "There wasn't enough family to fall apart in the first place."

"But . . . you miss having a family in any case."

"OK, yes, I do."

"I was thinking I might start you in my group," he said. "I had thought about this for some time—but you are so young. No one else in the group is younger than thirty-two."

"I'm nearly half their age."

He looked me over grimly.

"Do you think I could try it?"

Dr. Sternbach leaned his elbows on his knees. "Well, I will have to ask them first," he said. "And I will let you know."

He would allow me to come once—if they liked me, I could stay.

"Maybe you could be the youngest sister in the family," he said, raising his eyebrows.

I nodded. I saw myself surrounded by quietly nodding grownups who sat, chins in hands, listening and sympathizing.

That Thursday I went to Dr. Sternbach's apartment at nine in the evening. The group met from 9:15 to 10:45 in his living room—past that wrought-iron gate I had never yet entered, into that room crammed with Biedermeier sofas and armchairs, even a little round table. More books lined shelves, and oil paintings that I later found had been completed by Dr. Sternbach himself, Alpine scenes like something out of *The Sound of Music* hung in gold leaf frames. A hawk-nosed young man with an unsmiling face, a shock of brown hair falling thickly over his forehead, sat upright in his chair. His eyes had the piercing intensity I associated with Indian braves in Wild West films. He crossed his legs with the grace of a professional athlete. He nodded, which did not make him more forbidding, then did smile slightly—that made him handsome—and shook my hand.

"I'm Erik," he said in a deep voice. He looked strong, but also withdrawn. I hoped I could draw him out, help him, and I imagined him asking me out to dinner, although I realized that would be forbidden by Dr. Sternbach. The doorbell rang, and a woman and man were buzzed in. They greeted Erik briefly, turned to look at me, and hung their coats before coming in and sitting down.

"I'm Hannah," said the woman softly. She seemed not to want to be noticed, but she did smile at me. She wore a dark wool skirt that I liked and a gray turtleneck with a pale blue scarf, a Navajo turquoise ring ornamenting her forefinger, complementing a pair of matching earrings. She moved with easy grace, and I guessed her age at forty-five. Her short, graying hair frothed around her head in loose curls.

The man was much older—older than my parents. He looked like a professor, which is what he turned out to be. The other members arrived, two by two, and seated themselves in the circle. Only Dr. Sternbach was missing, and he entered with an air of princely rectitude. He sat down in a La-Z-Boy recliner identical to the one in his office and tilted it back.

"We have a new member," he began, "and I think each of you should introduce yourselves to her, tell how old you are, too, and explain the conflicts that sent you to the group."

I had butterflies in my stomach. What if my problems were trivial compared to theirs? What if they criticized me the way Dr. Sternbach did?

The herringbone-tweeded professorial type raised his hand. "I'll start," he said. "I'm Jay. I'm sixty-two, I'm married and have twins who are two. My wife and I are having some problems, but we are aware of them and working on them. That is, marital problems—"

Dr. Sternbach interrupted. "Yes, everybody here has *some problems*." He gestured impatiently at Jay. "Why don't you *say* what the problem is?" He jigged his foot impatiently.

"Well—," Jay hesitated.

"You are homosexual!" Dr. Sternbach exploded.

I restrained myself from turning my head to stare, but I wanted to do so. Out of the corner of my eye, I glanced at Jay while he was gazing at Dr. Sternbach and wondered why he looked so ordinary.

"But that's under control," Jay insisted. "I can sleep with my wife. And we're a family—we have twins."

Suddenly I spoke up. "You're homosexual?" I asked.

"Yes," Jay said. He looked me straight in the eye. He sounded definite.

"*You're* homosexual?"

"Yes."

"Wow!" I said. Jay actually smiled. I thought homosexuals looked different. The ones I had seen sashayed when they walked. They wore lavender T-shirts. "You're homosexual, but you have sex with your wife?" I couldn't imagine how. But I wanted to be able to do so.

"Of course!" Jay said.

"How does that work?" I asked. "I mean, are you able to do it if you really want to be with men?"

Jay stared past me for a moment, then smiled his sad little smile. "Well, the breasts get in the way."

I leaned forward, ready to continue on this fascinating topic, when Dr. Sternbach nodded to Erik, who said, "I'm thirty-one. I'm studying law. I enjoy mountain climbing."

Dr. Sternbach added that Erik enjoyed withdrawing from the world, and Erik nodded ruefully, insisting that he enjoyed mountains, being so high up he could see five states. Dr. Sternbach pointedly inquired with whom he went on his hikes. Erik scowled, muttering that he'd been through all that, adding that "Jenna" wasn't so athletic and couldn't walk as fast.

I noticed that Dr. Sternbach had a way of leaping on something a group member wanted to hide, the way he did with me.

I looked at Erik. "Is Jenna your girlfriend?"

Erik smiled. "Yes, but she wants to break up with me because I haven't taken her hiking. She thinks I'm seeing someone else."

"Actually, she is right. You *are* seeing someone else—yourself. You seem to have no room in your life for her," Dr. Sternbach intoned.

I was relieved that someone aside from me seemed to be in the hot seat. Others spoke up, including Hannah, who said, "And I'm the one who is always bursting into tears because he," she gestured at Dr. Sternbach, "doesn't understand me."

The room burst into laughter. I liked these people. They seemed interested in trying to tell the truth about themselves. Mom and Dad never did that, and usually they tried not to see problems unless the problems blew up in their faces. I loved the way everyone said exactly what he or she was thinking—nothing like my real family. I could see Mom's shocked expression, watching me sitting with a real homosexual on one side, a guy having weird sex with his girlfriend on the other. If she knew I were hearing this stuff, she'd freak. But all this would now be my secret.

"My brother set his room on fire yesterday," I said suddenly.

"Whoa! Fireworks! I like dis one!" Merv, a salesman, announced. He pointed at me. "She's dynamite!" he added, chuckling rather oafishly. I wasn't sure I liked Merv. I felt a little afraid of him. And I didn't like his New York accent. Emboldened by all the truth telling, I said so.

Nobody yelled. Nobody cried or looked upset. They smiled at me in a friendly, tolerantly encouraging way that made me feel ashamed, like a four-year-old caught peeing in her pants.

"You are supposed to say what you think here," Dr. Sternbach announced. "You go ahead. You tell everyone what you think of them." And I did. I told Erik he looked forbidding, and I told two other members that they sounded as though they came from Queens—the worst thing I could think of to say. I told Hannah that she seemed like she felt sorry for herself. I told another man that he ought to sit up straight—more women would probably be interested in him. Then I fell silent, horrified by my outburst. I hadn't said one nice thing about anybody, and I couldn't think of one good thing to say about myself.

The slouchy man actually sat up straight, learned forward, and smiled. "New blood!" he said. "I think we need it here. I'm glad you've come, Melissa."

I pulled at the sleeves of my sweater. I inserted a finger in the top of my turtleneck and hitched it up further, so that the tip of my chin was covered.

Merv looked me over. "Tell me about a typical day at your house, kid."

"A typical day?" No one had asked me that, not even Dr. Stern-bach. "My mother makes coffee, but you know she's making it because you hear her slamming pots and muttering 'damn,' and then you smell something burning. When you walk into the kitchen, there's a spray of brown on the kitchen wall—she always lets it perk 'til it splatters the wall. Then my father comes in and yells at her or teases her until she starts yelling back or pushing him out of the kitchen. He's bigger than she is, so she's not very successful. Once he took a pencil she liked and held it over his head and she jumped up and down trying to get it while he danced away from her and then all the toast burned and I didn't get any breakfast. My brother said why don't I just pour myself a bowl of Cheerios the way he does. He never fights with either of them. I hate my father."

I started to cry, and no one laughed. I started to feel that sense of nothingness, of falling into space where I fell forever and couldn't see or feel anything and there was a cold wind. Just falling and falling and falling. I tried to put that into words for them, and they all listened and said nothing until the very end of the session, when Marcia suddenly said what Dr. Sternbach had been telling me for months.

"It's just that you love your father so very much."

I liked the way they said nothing, waited a moment to let things sink in. My family talked constantly, or if they remained silent, it was only because menace was in the air and the next few seconds would bring a slap or a scream.

But the group's silence lasted only a few minutes. Merv broke it.

He leaned forward, slapped his knees. "So that's *breakfast* by you," he said. "How's about dinner?"

I laughed.

"At dinner, my brother and I shovel our food in quickly because we don't like the fights. Sometimes Dad makes us eat boiled okra, and my brother dumps his into a small drawer under the table. We ask to be excused until dessert. Dad really slammed his drink down a few nights ago and gin shot over the table. Mom jumped up and ran into the kitchen. We heard thumps, soft thumps. When I got to the kitchen door, rolls of paper towels were lying all over the floor, and my mom was throwing another one down. She said, 'I'm expressing anger!'"

"How do you get away from all that?" Hannah asked, looking concerned. "I mean, it all sounds so disturbing—"

"Well, I like to go to dance classes," I started. "I'm in ballet—"

"Ach," said Dr. Sternbach. "It's time." He pushed himself up from his La-Z-Boy. I got up with the others, and we walked out together.

EIGHT

Food Fights

> You don't get over hating to cook,
> any more than you get over having big feet.
>
> PEG BRACKEN, author of *The I Hate to Cookbook*

It was dinnertime, and I was setting the table with Dad's blue-and-white Canton china dishes. He loved them so much that he wouldn't let anyone else wash them—not even Macie. Every evening after dinner, he donned an apron, carefully stacked the Canton dishes, and took them into the kitchen. As he washed the dishes, he sang in a cheerfully slow singsong voice:

> Goddamn son of a bitch!
> Son of a, son of a, son of a bitch!
> Goddamn son of a bitch!
> Don't you touch my Canton China!
> Goddamn son of a bitch!
> Son of a, son of a, son of a . . .

From time to time he'd stop and titter or chortle, then go back to his dishes. After he'd washed them and let them dry in the drainer, he gave each plate a once-over with a clean dish towel and stashed them safely in the corner cupboard.

We had a big brass Indian dinner bell that Mom or I used every evening to summon everyone to dinner. Once I'd folded the napkins and put out the cutlery, I raised the dinner bell, as usual.

Only this time the bell slipped from my hands, landing, before I could catch it, in the middle of Dad's plate, splitting it in two. I stared a moment at the two halves of the plate, and I shook. Maybe we could glue them? The plate hadn't shattered but had broken into two distinct pieces. I thought of pushing the sides back together but felt afraid to touch them. I went into the kitchen, where Mom was humming as the kettle, now empty, continued to burn on the stove, the corn on the cob boiling away, turning to mush, the chicken looking dry, the rice undercooked.

"Mom?"

She started. "Yes, dearie?"

I told her about the plate. She sighed, turning off all the burners on the stove.

"I'll go in with you to tell Dad," she said. Wrapping her arms around herself as if she were cold, she accompanied me.

"*Goddamn it!*" he screamed at the two of us, his face contorted. He was sitting at his desk and slammed his fists down on it. We ran out, and the glass-paned doors of his music room banged shut. I heard crashing noises, as if things were being thrown at walls. I went to my room, closed the door. After about ten minutes, I opened it, but I could still hear Dad. A howl of agony, as if he'd fallen off a mountain and broken his leg in four places, then, "Goddamn bitch! Oh, Lord! *Bitch*! Why can't we ever have anything *nice*?"

Mom loved paper plates and insisted we use them for birthday parties and picnics. Dad hated them, and secretly I went along with him. I loved the patterns and colors of his blue-and-white china. Sometimes we went on expeditions to Chinatown, where he found one or two Canton pieces and my brother and I got fried dough delights called honeybows—but it was rare that Dad found any plates. He haunted flea markets on weekends but never found china, though he did gleefully return with some blue-and-white Delft. I doubted he could replace the broken plate.

I padded into the kitchen, rummaged through the fridge, taking out butter, honey, ice cream. "You don't want to ruin your dinner, dearie," Mom said vaguely. She was holding up a box of rice, apparently scrutinizing the instructions. Several boxes of frozen broccoli were piled near her, and she was squeezing them and muttering something.

I took the food back to my room. I dipped crackers in a hunk of butter and honey and kept eating, even though I was full. I went back to the bathroom, locked the door, and, while flushing the toilet so I wouldn't be heard, stuck my finger down my throat and vomited. I flushed again, opened a window, brushed my teeth, washed my hands, and went back to my room. I felt strange but calmer. It was a relief to get all that weight off my stomach.

Dinner was late that night, but we did eat, Dad on a different Canton plate, the food overcooked—typical for a meal Mom had prepared. We ate in near silence, Dad with a tumbler of gin in his hand, until Mom said, "Maybe you'd like the news?"

Dad turned without speaking and switched on the TV. Congresswoman Bella Abzug, in one of her gigantic hats, was shaking her fists and yelling into the microphone in front of a large crowd of people holding antiwar banners.

"Stop the *war*! Sign the peace agreement! Because of the *war*, because of the death of our boys in Vietnam, I do impeach the *president of the United States*!" Massive applause.

Dad hissed, leaned forward, snapped the TV back off, took a swig of his drink and set the tumbler down on the table hard. He jabbed at his food with his fork.

"That goddamn Bella Abzug! I'd like to tear her arms off and beat her brains out with them!" He stood up from the table, taking his plate into the kitchen. He did not sing but went into his music room, slamming the door.

Mom adjusted her place mat and nodded at me and Roland. "Phew!" she said, smiling brightly, leaning back in her chair with an air of aplomb and looking at us expectantly. We said nothing. She leaned forward and spread her hands on the table.

"Dad's identified with Richard Nixon, you see. That's why he acts like that. He can't stand any criticism of the president because it feels like *he* is being criticized. Do you understand?" She leaned forward on her elbows, gazing at both of us to see if we'd taken in her words, then sighed several times—panted, really, as if she were carrying a load, but her eyes shone as if she were excited and she was rocking her head, as if keeping time to a song.

Roland stared straight ahead. I was pretty sure he hadn't heard her.

"May I please be excused?" I asked. Mom nodded, looking disappointed, and I went to my room. I knew she wanted me to say something bad about Dad, and I didn't want to talk.

I went to Dr. Sternbach the next day and sat in the chair opposite his La-Z-Boy, as I had for my first few sessions. He picked up a folded napkin—I saw he had a pile of them on the side of the couch's headpiece—and spread it out. Gesturing to the couch, he said, "You should lie down to talk. That is analysis."

I liked the bright red Aztec couch covering but felt that moving to the couch meant being too far away from Dr. Sternbach. If I lay down on the couch, I wouldn't be able to see his face, and I liked being able to see his face. I said so.

"Ah!" He raised a finger. "Freud had patients lie on the couch just so they could not see his face. He needed the freedom to react without having the patient judge his facial expression all the time. *That* is analysis!"

I lay down on the couch. To my right, the army of Egyptian figurines marched toward Dr. Sternbach. At my feet, the Hindu and African masks on the bookcase and wall opposite looked ready to swallow me.

"The masks are scary," I said.

"Good! Just say what comes to mind! What is scary?" asked Dr. Sternbach's voice. "You say whatever comes to mind." What scared me was not knowing what Dr. Sternbach might say and do. He could see me and I couldn't see him. That was scary. But I didn't mention this.

Still, he sounded interested in me. That reassured me.

My vomiting seemed too embarrassing to mention. Lately I'd been scribbling down the caloric content of everything I ate and adding it up. I couldn't eat an egg and a piece of toast without thinking *egg, seventy calories, plus toast, about a hundred, plus butter, maybe fifty.* I totaled everything at the end of the day, trying to keep from eating more than fifteen hundred calories. Every few days I gorged on pretzels and ice cream or chocolate syrup, then made myself throw up. But I told him all about the dinner bell, the plate, Dad's screaming, and Bella Abzug, whom I'd heard mentioned at school. My teachers liked her.

"*Ja,* your father is an alcoholic!" Dr. Sternbach said. "Psychotic, too."

"You mean Dad's crazy?"

"Crazy, yes, he is crazy. Alcoholic and psychotic. Probably paranoid."

It had never occurred to me that Dad was crazy. I thought of him as angry, although he could be sweet to me, especially if Mom wasn't there. I liked the sound of the terms Dr. Sternbach had used, which I hadn't heard, and which seemed to mean something important. To explain meant to understand, to understand, to fix. The minute I got home, I found Mom in the living room, bent over a letter she was writing.

"Mom, is Dad an alcoholic? Psychotic, too?"

Mom looked up, surprised. "No, he's not!" I hadn't expected her to act annoyed. Maybe she thought I hadn't noticed his drinking? Or that the drinking wasn't so bad?

"But, I thought, I mean the way he drinks—"

Mom shoved her letter aside. She tapped the table with the end of her pen, set the envelope near the letter, and, looking me in the eye, said, "Dr. Berkeley told me he is a *problem drinker,* not an alcoholic. She tested him and he is not psychotic *at all.*"

I was about to say he got all red in the face every night, but Mom spoke again.

"He also has a high IQ! That was tested, too!" Mom said, and I knew better than to say more.

In my next session, Dr. Sternbach told me to sit in the chair again.

"Listen: everything you say in here is private." He touched his chest. "I don't repeat what *you* say." He pointed at me, Uncle Sam style: "*You* don't repeat what *I* say either." He nodded seriously. "Otherwise, it becomes very difficult to work together, you understand?" He spread his hands.

I understood.

"I don't talk to anybody about *you,* and you don't repeat to your parents or anyone else what we say to each other in this room. *That* is analysis! Now lie down on the couch."

A few weeks later, his uniform-clad Viennese maid, a kindly, bustling figure, the source of the wonderful aromas in the kitchen I inhaled before each session, and who smiled at me whenever she happened to open the kitchen door, pressed an object wrapped in a damp paper towel into my hands as I sat waiting for my session.

"Doctor's proud of you for getting better in school!" she said. "Here's a seed, a seed from an avocado. You can grow it at home in a pot, OK?" She smiled.

I packed the seed away in my schoolbag and didn't mention it to Dr. Sternbach. I wanted to keep and plant what she had given me—I knew Dad would help me, too. He had many plants on the windowsills, watered them daily and fertilized them. His begonias, rubber trees, fig trees, flourished, and I knew he would enjoy mixing the soil and finding the right pot for the avocado seed.

In the next session, however, I did mention to Dr. Sternbach that his maid seemed to know about my schoolwork.

Dr. Sternbach shrugged. "It is not important. She is just the maid."

"But you told me never to talk to anybody—"

"*Ach!*" He waved a hand at me, an affronted look flashing across his face. "This is not important. Your *analysis* is important. Lie down on the couch."

I lay there and looked up at that Hindu mask that always seemed about to leap off the wall and chew me up.

"What are you thinking?"

"Nothing."

"Remember, you must say whatever comes to mind, no matter what."

I thought of myself eating and then throwing up, but I didn't feel like telling him that. I sighed. Then I thought of something I wanted to talk about. School photos had just been taken. I thought he would like to see them. I was wearing my favorite gray Peruvian sweater with the white llamas. I showed him the photo.

He tapped it and shook his head. "Yes, I see you are a narcissist. You want everyone to look at you."

I felt my face burning.

"You are right here in the middle of the line, wanting to be the center of attention. Exhibitionistic. You want everyone to see this sweater, and it's a boring sweater. I want you to develop style! I want you to be a lady!"

I took the photo back and looked. I had not noticed where I was standing, only that I was enjoying myself, standing with a friend, that I felt I had one or two friends now. And I didn't think I looked ugly in the picture. I put the photo in my bookbag. I had liked the sweater, but I wouldn't wear it now.

"You want to get well, don't you? You want to get rid of your problems?"

"Yes."

"Then you must say everything that comes to mind, no matter how strange it sounds or how embarrassing."

Suddenly, lying there, I remembered I'd told two girls in my jazz dance class something Hannah in my group had said. I'd used her first name. I felt nauseous with guilt; I told Dr. Sternbach I felt guilty that I'd repeated something Hannah said.

"You must keep things in the group private!" he thundered. "Otherwise we cannot help you!"

I got the idea that reporting embarrassing things would make me well. And many things embarrassed me—I knew I was considered a weirdo, and I had few friends. I knew my friends' parents didn't like my parents. I told Dr. Sternbach about how I counted calories and occasionally vomited.

"You must stop this at once! At once!" A fist slammed down on the couch by my head, so close to my ear that I jumped.

"I don't want to gain weight. I've been going to ballet classes, you know, and jazz." I wanted to tell him how much I loved those classes.

"This is psychotic behavior, this vomiting!" He shook his head angrily. "Dancers. They are all crazy, psychotic. Anorexics. You want to be like *that*?"

"I don't like to throw up—I just do it sometimes when I have eaten too much. Dancers are thin—I don't yet have that kind of thinness."

69

"Stop it at once! Now! This is nothing but a substitute for orgasm."

I sat up and looked at him. He was red in the face. "Lie back down on the couch!" he yelled.

I did.

"Say what comes to mind!"

I thought of Mom walking beside me on Broadway, a pained expression on her face, suddenly doing high ballet kicks for no particular reason that I could see. Her leg whammed upward so forcefully that a person standing in her way would have been knocked unconscious.

"Whee!" she said, with each kick. People stared. I walked ahead of her, hoping not to be noticed.

"Your mother has a constant need to be freeing herself," Dr. Sternbach observed, when I had finished.

I couldn't have put it better. I felt immense relief. He did know what I was talking about! He did believe me! I lay there, suddenly relaxed, looking at the many-colored books lining his shelves. A whole row of red books—I wondered what those were. Huge art books. It would be nice to go over there and take them down one by one and look at them.

But even though he understood me, Dr. Sternbach didn't know Mom, I realized. If you were a drunk lying on your side with a few flies buzzing over your smelly body, my mother would love you. She would find you and she would love you. You'd be sleeping peacefully in a subway car, and she'd come up from behind, tap you somewhere inappropriate, and say, "Oh? Excuse me? Do you need anything?" Sometimes she held out a dollar bill or a chocolate bar, and cheered, as if for a favorite team, when it was accepted.

Certain that Dr. Sternbach was encouraging me to say what I felt, I went ahead and did so.

"She's *always* doing those high kicks on the street, like some chorus girl. Like she wants people to see her do that. She won't stop doing that, even though I asked her to."

"Do you *know* why you dislike your mother?"

I sat up on the couch and twisted my head around to see his expression, which looked ominous. I felt thrust off-balance. He seemed to be saying there was something I had missed about why I disliked my mother. But I thought I knew why: she expected me to admire or reassure her all the time, liked to pretend that she was the little girl and I was the mean mother—I was just getting warmed up talking about how she couldn't cook, let my father—

Dr. Sternbach interrupted me. "Do you *know* why?" he repeated.

I fell silent, since he wanted another answer, and I didn't have it.

"Because you are so dependent on her!"

I was? I lay on the couch filled with horror. I wanted to get away from her, to be nothing like her. He seemed to be saying I was connected to her, as if by an umbilical cord.

"Your mother is *generous*! You have no idea what it is to have children, to care for them. No idea at all."

I had nothing to say. That was true—I had no idea about being a mother.

"You are spoiled! A terrible child. You should be grateful to your mother for all she has done for you."

"But . . ." I looked at those masks and felt a shiver. "She's, somehow, so childish." I braced myself. The fist slammed down again, right by my ear.

"So she's childish!"

I sat up again.

Dr. Sternbach cast me an exasperated look, tapped on the arm of his La-Z-Boy.

"Don't you see that you *must* have a good relationship with your mother? Otherwise *you will not be able to have good relationships at all*. If you cannot build a relationship with her, you cannot build *any* relationships. You want friends, you want boyfriends. Well, start at home—with your mother."

"But she doesn't listen—she does all kinds of strange things."

"You are an idiot! Like most teenagers, you think only of yourself. You don't think what your mother goes through or what she feels."

Thump! Thump! His fist hit the couch. He sounded absolutely sure of himself, and I saw that my bad relationship with Mom was my fault, that if I didn't fix the problem, I'd never have a relationship with a boy or anyone else. I hoped desperately there might be some way around this problem. Dr. Sternbach was muttering under his breath.

"Spoiled!" he said, so that I could hear him. "You are just a spoiled brat."

In a journal entry written after one year of psychotherapy, I wrote, "A girl was unable to express certain feelings to her analyst because she believed they were beyond the realm of his experience (cultural & otherwise). To enable herself to communicate with him she adopted his values and ethics, abandoned hers. She became his moral shadow."

That girl on the couch knew what she was talking about. But I barely gave her the time of day.

NINE

Diagnosis

Ladybird, ladybird, fly away home
MOTHER GOOSE

I lay on Sternbach's couch.

"What do you want?" he said, clearing his throat as though he were planning on spitting in my direction. I could hear the squashy noises his body made as he shifted his weight around in his La-Z-Boy, pumping air pockets in the old leather, and I could picture his impatient expression. I assumed he felt angry because of something I'd done wrong or was failing to do right.

"I want to find myself," I said.

The cool kids were always saying that, the ones who emerged from our all-girls school into the arms of waiting boys, the girls who wore Mexican peasant blouses, landlubber bell-bottoms, and blue clogs.

"What are you gonna do? Look down on the floor and *find* yourself?" He pointed down to his Persian carpet. Under his breath he muttered, "Oh, *veh*."

I was lying on the red couch staring up at the African masks with the huge, pronged noses wondering whether my friends liked me, and if so, why on earth they did. Would I pass ninth grade? I was failing math, as usual.

I showed Dr. Sternbach a poem I'd written in what I imagined to be the style of Dorothy Parker.

He sat reading, a grumpy look on his face. The minutes dragged as he silently cast his eyes over my short poem. I looked around the office as he read, wishing and hoping he would like my poem, or find some good in it.

Finally he looked up from the poem, proclaiming, "Dorothy Parker had wit! Dorothy Parker had style! *You* cannot write in the style of Dorothy Parker," as if I were too great a nonentity even to read Parker, let alone try to write like her.

I retreated into the urgent question of finding myself, and the fist slammed down on the couch again, the voice behind me trumpeting, "You have to *work,* and then you will find yourself *in your work.*"

I loved writing, so maybe it did not count. I had the feeling that to qualify as work, an activity had to feel onerous. I had the analyst on record as saying "*your* work is your schoolwork!" and English remained one of the few subjects I was not failing. Whenever I wrote a paper for one of my English teachers, I felt I could belong someday to their world of people who knew how to write. Or maybe I thought of them as mothers who approved of me, unlike my own.

By the time I left, I felt I could succeed at nothing.

I stood on the corner of 96th Street and Central Park West, a few feet from Sternbach's building. Instead of turning left and walking to Broadway, where I normally took the subway home, I turned right onto Central Park West. It was a cold, late afternoon in October. The very few people on the sidewalk seemed to be hurrying home for dinner. Brown and red leaves swirled at my feet, and I did up the toggles of my blue duffle coat.

I wanted to show Dr. Sternbach how smart I was but could find no way. I shifted from one foot to the other, running through my repertoire looking for something new: when I talked about the Alvin Ailey company dancing *Revelations*, Sternbach demanded that I "reveal" something. He'd interrupted my account of seeing the New York City Ballet to say that I should forget about that and see some opera. Opera was real art. Dance was just—he didn't use a word, even—he waved his hand as if to push away the thought. Fade haircuts, tie-dye T-shirts, landlubber bell-bottoms, psychedelic designs, Robin Morgan's *Sisterhood Is Powerful* anthology, had all elicited contempt. He had told me about a paper he was writing on the American Declaration of Independence, with its delusional (he said) phrases like "pursuit of happiness." The moment I heard that phrase, I dared not tell him how much I liked it.

Racking my brain for a topic that might find favor, I heard a voice—a male voice, a male Hispanic voice, hissing and whispering. An old white Chevy Nova was idling on the corner. Had I put out my thumb? I dreamed of hitchhiking—I'd wanted to go to Woodstock that way the year before but had chickened out.

Now was my chance.

The man in the car beckoned.

"Hey, babeeee," he crooned. As if on automatic pilot, I walked over to the two-door car and climbed in. The inside reeked of cigarette smoke. A couple of plush cubes, dice, dangled from the rearview mirror. I felt exhilarated for the second that it took me to open the car door and sit down: now I was bold, now I was free, now I was the author of my fate. That was what half of me felt. The other half was somehow not there, or sleeping, or looking to the left. I was in a dazed state that seemed vaguely familiar, and still, I was telling myself I had just taken charge.

Except that the man turned and smiled and his face fell. I thought he, too, found me ugly, but he muttered something I didn't understand under his breath.

"You like spic guys, girlie?" he asked. His voice was gravelly, and I had no idea what he was talking about, so I said nothing. He drove north on Central Park West, and I started to feel scared when I looked out the window and nothing looked familiar. We were driving in an area I'd never seen, a beat-up, poorer part of the Upper West Side.

"Would you please take me to 110th and Broadway?" I could hear my voice shaking and told myself not to cry.

"Hey, girlie, how old are you?"

I didn't answer.

"I take you there, you gotta kiss me at least."

I said OK. My heart was hammering, and I found it hard to breathe. He looked a lot older than I'd first thought. Maybe even forty. He was jigging one knee, and suddenly he patted my hand, grabbed it. His hand felt rough.

"You just a baby, ain't you?"

"I'm not a baby!"

"Yeah, yeah, yeah." He chuckled. He pulled up to the north side of 110th Street and stopped.

"Come on, baby. One kiss." Certain I had no choice, I let him kiss me. His lips were soft but chapped, and he stuck his tongue, which tasted of cigarettes, into my mouth. I let him do that for a moment and then pulled back. He glanced at me as if wondering whether I'd like more. I opened the car door, almost forgetting my schoolbag, jumped out, and ran up Broadway toward my corner. Whirling through my head were indoor images—the now cozier-than-ever consulting room in Dr. Sternbach's apartment, my own family's living room with the worn green paisley couch, the dark, stuffy ancestor portraits that suddenly seemed warm, welcoming. The inside of the car alternated in my mind with those warm rooms where nothing bad could happen. I stopped running on 111th Street and entered a grocery store. Just moving in the direction of the display cases soothed me. I picked up a Dannon coffee yogurt and a stick of butter. I would buy those. I took them to the cashier, paid, and left.

When I arrived home, I expected Mom to ask why I was late. I was trying to prepare some innocuous answer—the subway stalled, I decided to walk, I lost track of time because I was browsing, looking at the cards in the stationery store—but Mom just said, "Hello, dearie," as if nothing were out of the ordinary. I nodded and walked back to my room. I looked at my clock. I wasn't late. I was home earlier than usual. Everything in the world had happened, but I was home on time.

Suddenly I wondered what I would tell Dr. Sternbach. My adventure had seemed like a good idea. Since I'd lived to tell the tale, I started trying to convince myself nothing could touch me. Except that I kept floating back down to a sense of everything being all wrong—gray, black, and wrong. My worst fear had always been that I'd end up a bag lady on the street with my shopping bags filled with clothes and strange objects that bag ladies keep. I'd spend my days just sitting on the sidewalk with a plastic cup in front of me, hoping somebody would give me enough to buy a cheese sandwich and a cup of coffee.

I'd rather worry about that.

I went into my room, closed the door, and lay down on my bed. My heart was pounding, and lying on my bed without moving didn't seem to change anything. I sat up, touched my pillow, and muttered, "This is a pillow." I took my phone off the hook, listened to the dial tone, and murmured, "This is a phone." I wanted to convince myself that my room and my surroundings were as real as the inside of that car, and I almost succeeded in doing so until I opened my journal and found that all I could write was "I am alive," before feeling myself choke up.

I did tell Dr. Sternbach the whole story. He sat very still and said nothing. Finally, he murmured, "You know, it may just be too dangerous for me to treat you."

This panicked me. "What?"

"If you want to do things like this, it is your life, not mine. But I am not sure that I want to continue treating you."

I started to sob. Soon I was crying so hard I was afraid I might throw up. He spoke again, and his voice seemed kind.

"I want to help people who want to get well. Not people who want to harm themselves. What you did climbing into the car of a stranger was . . . don't you realize that at the very least, you could have been raped?"

Having him talk about it made me relive feeling trapped, having no idea what would happen, knowing I was in the strange man's power and too scared not to do whatever he said. The kiss had been horrible—I washed my mouth out with Listerine when I got home. I was terrified that Dr. Sternbach would throw me out of treatment, and he made me promise not to do anything like that ever again—as if I would ever want to do so.

I didn't sleep well. The last thing he had said was that he would like for me to "go for tests" so he could better help me.

I was impossible. He didn't know what to do with me. Maybe I was psychotic.

"Tests that show how you think and feel. An IQ test as well."

"An IQ test?" That scared me. What if the test showed that I was dumb?

"That is the least important aspect of it. I want to help you figure out why you do things that are dangerous. Do you have any idea why you got in the car of this man?"

None that I'd admit to myself, and least of all to him. "It seemed like a good idea at the time."

"But why?"

I shrugged. "I thought I was taking control. I'd have some wild, free experience." Just saying it made me cringe. How ridiculous. I was ridiculous, just as he said.

I went for testing on a mild fall day that started sunny but became overcast halfway through the afternoon. When I left school around three, clouds had kicked up and it was sprinkling; by the time I got to the bus stop, it was pouring, and by the time I'd gotten off and walked to 300 Central Park West, I was soaked. The doorman cast his eyes over me disapprovingly. At fifteen, I didn't appreciate the art deco façade, or the reputation enjoyed by the twin-towered edifice for housing New York's most prestigious analysts. But the looming green awning with the building's name, "The Eldorado," the gigantic pots of flowers on either side of the door, gave the place the aura of a temple.

Exiting the elevator at the fifteenth floor, I was greeted by a bland woman in a knit suit. Offering me a towel, she led me into a spacious apartment with ten-foot ceilings, hardwood floors, and oversized windows. I dried off, accepted a cup of hot tea, and followed her into her office, where she sat across from me looking me over from head to toe. She scanned me as if I were a specimen she planned to dissect. I thought of the earthworms pinned to wax boards that my class had to cut up in biology.

The psychologist showed me a series of strange pictures—a boy with a sad face playing a violin, a woman in an armchair with a man lurking behind the chair—and asked me to make up stories. There were inkblots and something I thought was probably an IQ test, where I had to examine geometric shapes and explain what they'd look like if they were folded into boxes. I was sure I'd failed, but the woman's voice and face remained resolutely neutral. When I asked at the end how I'd done, she smiled, it seemed to me, an insincere smile. I had already inquired three or four times whether my IQ was OK.

She laughed, showing tobacco-stained teeth, and held my gaze with tired, slightly sad eyes that had laugh wrinkles, but said nothing. She seemed to be tabulating data. Her face said "crazy," but it also, I realized years later, said regret, or perhaps resignation. Perhaps she felt sorry for me. She had made her diagnosis, which seemed as set as the lines in her face. Having completed the puzzle, she was done. I wonder whether she would have felt differently had I been able to sit her down and say, "Listen, lady—I don't need tests! I need to get away from my parents and my brother! I don't know where to go! *Please,* help me get away!" A scientist examining a drop of blood on a slide, she had typed me.

When I arrived for a session a week or so after the tests, Dr. Sternbach was holding the business envelope containing my results. He sat flipping through the report, holding those five pages of single-spaced ten-point type so that I could not see them, declaiming a few phrases: how I'd arrived "literally drenched" and had "an otherworldly Burne-Jones quality," a term he had to explain, getting down one of his art history tomes to show me Pre-Raphaelite paintings. Burne-Jones painted a naked Andromeda chained to a rock who is rescued—just before a monster eats her—by a Perseus tricked out in a stylish suit of armor.

No Perseus was to come my way.

The beauties in these paintings had pale faces, sad eyes with big lashes, and thick, curly hair that tumbled around them, Godiva-style.

I was like that? Pretty?

Dr. Sternbach looked startled. "Yes, you are a very pretty girl," he answered in a factual tone.

        The Rorschach like the other tests, indicates an acutely
traumatic family background, one that must be marked by constant up-
heaval. In a poignant way, Melissa describes her loneliness, lack of
secure emotional attachments, regressive goals. Disappointment and
distrust are reflected in past narcissistic deprivation. This gifted girl
gives ample evidence of her unfulfilled oral dependency needs. She
refers to "babies lying down". Oedipal figures are "Drawings by Dr. Seuss".
Male figures have phobic and paranoid elaborations. She makes much of their "eyes"
and assaultive potential. "Godzilla" or "A big monster, his tail hanging
behind him, he goes around stomping on things . . . witch 's claws . . .
I look up to it." Seductive and physical violence are incre___
blot. In part, her pa___

        Her ___   MELISSA KNOX   Page Two
oral sadistic objects,
biting into blood." Or   fantasy ridden intelligence with a schizophrenic thinking disorder.
inferiority, emphasis c   Pathological features are also present in her numerous discrepancies
aggressive ambivalences   and fluctuations in the Wechsler. Her poor concentration must filter down
assigned to her bizarre   to the classroom. She fumbled through the Arithmetic Reasoning with
and that looks like a m   erratic success. Her Memory reflects an obsessive anxiety pattern,
of melancholy . . . als   9 digits forward, a perfect score, but only 3 reversed. Impaired attention
                           appears also in her below average Digit Symbol score. Her anxiety about
        Meliss   time limits slowed her down in visual motor tasks. Her most serious
prefaced them with her c   deficiency on the Wechsler appears in the Picture Completion, another
if I have a low I.Q." :   indication of her weakened reality differentiation. Her less impaired
disturbance that is ref   functions include an above average conceptual ability and verbal
on the Wechsler. Learni   Comprehension. However, the latter is coupled with regressive tendencies
castration components.   on an acting out level.
friend or her lover." N
and in her competitive s
the like. Marital tensi   Her Information is average but uneven, with significant
that Melissa has been ex   ___borations. She didn't know who discovered the North Pole, a not
                           ___ she added, "There were two people." When she was unsure
                                          ___'t find it first." When she was unsure
                                                    ___telligence." In order
                                                          ___ment and regressive
                                                          ___d, "I won't run
                                                          ___ell people there
                                                          ___as quickly as

                300 CENTRAL PARK WEST
                NEW YORK, N.Y. 10024

                    212 724 144.
                                                          ___in her meticulous
PSYCHOLOGICAL EXAMINATION   ___an usual adolescent
    10/25/71   ___overing fragment
                                                          ___rked male-female
Referred by: Dr. Oscar Sternbach   MELISSA KNOX   ___tstretched. He
                                          Birthdate: 1/24/57 She could not
                                                          ___and feet, but she
Tests: Wechsler Bellevue Intelligence Scale   ___yes have an
            Verbal Scale   ___n.
            Performance Scale
            Full Scale   I.Q. 116   ___e to go to a free
       Rorschach   I.Q. 100   ___'t go there. I'd
       Thematic Apperception   I.Q. 108   ___ike to know a few
       Figure Drawings   ___o what I want to do."
       Bender Gestalt Drawings   ___al experience with a boy,
                                                          ___t. I'd like to go to
                                                          ___ family." Her Most
        Melissa is an attractive adolescent with long blond hair,   ___my father, and I hate
striking grey eyes, a fair skin, braces on her teeth, bitten nails. She
has an other worldly Burne-Jones quality. Her clothes were peer app-   ___ing in Melissa's
ropriate but the top of her blue work shirt was fastened by a pin. She   ___breaks in reality
arrived in the rain and she was literally drenched. Apparently she had   ___of fantasy. When the
sought no means of protection, and her face and clothes were wringing wet.   ___r superior intelligence,
She is an appealing, talkative, seriously disturbed girl with visible   ___ags. Chronic confusions
affect hunger and a naive confiding approach. Her I.Q. is invested with magic mean-   ___puberty. Her emotional
ing and she asked about this in the preliminaries. She has a depressive quality   ___al, impaired object
and her anxious giggles were interspersed with sighs. Occasionally she cracked   ___not provide adequate
her knuckles, or clicked her nails against her braces.   ___ear on a latent level,

        Melissa is in the ninth grade at Brearley where she's been since   ___t small details.
the first grade. She said she always does badly in Math and Science. She just
failed Geometry. She hates this school and she is very eager to change to
Collinsbrook in Maine. This is, "A free school that operates on the Summerhill
principle . . . they have only 46 kids." She hopes to become "a psychoanalyst
or a psychologist, or a lay analyst in Orgonomy . . . William Reich . . . I'm
interested in it, but I don't know if I want to have anything to do with it,
or I'd like to be an art teacher in a free school." Her leisure time
activities are solitary. "I take care of my guinea pigs and I make candles and
I read a lot."

        The total test impression is that of a schizophrenic but
salvageable girl with many assets. However, her background as it appears in
her projective responses, suggests that she may represent one aspect of a
family pathology. In this regard, the prognostic outlook is less optimistic.
Her environment as she describes it, does not seem conducive to maturational
growth and effective reality testing.

        Melissa's Wechsler I.Q.'s measure her functioning level
rather than her intellectual ability. The Rorschach reveals a superior but

"What did the psychologist *say* about me? Can't I read that?"

"No, that is written for me. But I can tell you that she does like you, that you seemed to her all torn apart."

"Is that what she wrote?"

He sighed, as if weighing how much to tell me.

"I want to know what she wrote!"

He looked me in the eye. "She describes you as severely disturbed, but salvageable."

"That sounds like I'm really crazy." I asked if I would get well.

"You will always be a somewhat difficult girl," he offered. With a great deal of time on the couch, I might be "salvaged." I felt like an old car at the bottom of a junkyard heap.

By the time Sternbach was done rattling the pages of the document, shaking his head at my IQ, which he called "average" in a tone implying "moron," and raising his eyebrows at the diagnosis he declined to reveal but implied he'd bowdlerized, I had decided to forgo all disagreement. I was so sick that he was my only chance, and if I did not listen to him, terrible things would happen to me. My brother, at this time in seventh grade, was flunking out of school and spending long hours in his room, where he still had a collection of creatures which he called "oogums" and "psychums," made of cement and pipe cleaners, some with Dad's help. Roland told me they were alive and could hear him. Dad, meanwhile, had nightly rages at the dinner table and in front of the evening news: "That goddamn bitch Gloria Steinem! She oughta be horsewhipped! The communists are taking over!" I didn't want to end up like either Roland or Dad, certainly not like Mom. So I would listen to Dr. Sternbach. Forever. No matter what I thought—and I often found his ideas strange—I would force myself to agree, and I would go along with anything he wanted, so I'd be salvaged. The test meant that if I were to refuse doing Sternbach's bidding, I would become like my father, a man who saw enemies everywhere; like my mother, a woman so childlike "you couldn't seduce her if you tried," said one of her friends. Worst of all, I would be another lost soul wandering in a sea of drugs and delusions, like my brother. If I stayed with Sternbach, who insisted that "maybe" if he had worked with my brother for years, Roland could have been saved, too, I might have a chance.

"Everyone in my family is crazy," I told him more than once.

The way was now clear. I was to come to Sternbach to avoid becoming crazy. Even more crazy.

TEN

Aborted

Strephon kissed me in the spring,
Robin in the fall,
But Colin only looked at me
And never kissed at all.
Strephon's kiss was lost in jest,
Robin's lost in play,
But the kiss in Colin's eyes
Haunts me night and day.

SARA TEASDALE, "The Look"

Tall, skinny Walt was sitting on my friend Meg's bed when I went to her house one afternoon. He was crooning to himself; he had been to elementary school with her, they both said. I thought he must be her boyfriend.

The phone rang as soon as I got home.

"Walt likes you."

"Me?"

The next afternoon, I met Walt in Riverside Park. At least a foot taller than me, his light brown hair falling to his shoulders, he wore black high-top sneakers and an air of guarded confidence. He smelled of cigarettes and pot. We walked in the park and he kissed me, and I liked the way he did so. With a view of the Hudson River and the Palisades across the way in New Jersey, we ambled along, holding hands, all the way to my house. My mother wasn't home, and I made him hot chocolate. We sat in the kitchen and drank it, and he kissed me until my lips felt swollen, then consumed most of the contents of our refrigerator, which wasn't quite enough. Perhaps I made him an English muffin. Decades later I was to learn that Walt's father kept no food in their house, that his mother occasionally visited and left a few bags of groceries. Walt liked me, even fell for me, but was even more attracted to my refrigerator. Walt was starving.

We met almost every day after school. He told me he'd been thrown out of the local parochial school in fourth grade for saying "damn." Actually, he confessed some years later, he was the worst behaved child in the school, such that the reverend mother used to find him and grip his arm during fire drills. He'd gone to public schools, an alternative high school, and the Columbia College Reading Room, where he picked up girls and scrounged for food in their refrigerators.

We were sitting on my bed talking when Dad knocked on the door. Before he entered, Walt and I jumped apart, but we were still sitting on my bed. Dad came in with some folded towels—when had he ever done laundry? Seeing us, he was so startled that he lifted the towel on top, dangling it from his hand like a woman trying to cover herself as he backed out the door.

"Here, uh, sweetie," said Dad, exiting with the towels.

Walt smiled. "Quite the southern gentleman, your father, isn't he?"

My mother poked her head in. She looked daggers, but spoke none.

This inclined me more and more to do what Walt wanted to do—have sex. I knew one girl who had had sex, and she'd warned me, "It feels like a Coke bottle going in."

Walt and I had enjoyed a number of afternoons kissing on his bed, and he was growing more and more eager. On a balmy afternoon a few months after we'd met, I watched him play basketball with his friends in Riverside Park and held his wallet for him when he asked. Inside was a condom. He said he'd been saving it a long time. He'd been saving it for *me*. I was impressed.

I didn't know that when you save a condom in a wallet for a long time, stick the wallet in the back pocket of your jeans and sit on the wallet daily, the condom rubs against the wallet. When the already-weakened latex contends with a maidenhead, rupture is likely.

The Coke bottle simile came to me as Walt pressed his way in; pain, not pleasure, accompanied his movements, and then all of a sudden everything seemed much better. I wasn't anywhere near orgasm, but I got the gist of the experience, until Walt pulled out and saw the tattered remnants of the condom.

"When did you have your last period?"

"About two weeks ago—why?"

Walt panicked before I did, since my knowledge of twenty-eight-day cycles was nonexistent, but we called Planned Parenthood right away. I wanted a pregnancy test and a diaphragm; instead, in a roomful of potato chip–crunching pregnant thirteen-year-olds, we were offered counseling on how not to get pregnant. Some of the girls in the room hated each other and wielded sharp objects because they were pregnant by the same guy. I got up, went to the desk, and demanded a nurse.

I did get a diaphragm fitting and was told when I could come back for a pregnancy test if I didn't get my period.

The next day, one of those New York spring days when warm wind swirls grit around your ankles before lapsing into torpid humidity, I stood in the phone booth on 116th Street and Riverside Drive hoping my mother would not walk by. I didn't dare call from home, three blocks away, in case she overheard, or listened at doors.

I would have to wait about twelve more days to learn whether I was pregnant. Maybe even two weeks. If I had to wait longer than that, I probably wouldn't be getting my period at all. I'd be pregnant. The thought made me dizzy with fear. I dialed Dr. Sternbach's number.

"Oh, *vey*, oh, *vey*!" He sounded furious. "You call your doctor!" he yelled. "Call *him*!"

Until I called the only doctor I knew, my pediatrician, I feared I would not be let back into Sternbach's office. I stuck a dime in the slot and dialed. Our pediatrician tended to roll his eyes at my mother, calling us "the crazy Knoxes." On my last visit, when I was fourteen, he'd embarrassed me by calmly intoning, "Now, if you masturbate, use something durable, don't use a test tube—we had a girl in the emergency room who'd done that."

As I listened in that three-walled booth to my pediatrician's phone ringing, a wind gusted off the Hudson River, blowing leaves over me. I pushed my head right into the small space on one side of the phone, trying to hide.

In his bland, unruffled voice, the doctor who had given me my immunizations and allergy shots, proclaiming on annual visits that I was "skinny as a rail—but healthy!" said, "Now, Melissa, you should see a good gynecologist."

"I went to Planned Parenthood!"

"Do you have a pencil?" He was speaking very slowly, possibly to calm me down. "Don't worry—I'll wait. I can send you to my wife's gynecologist."

"I'm going back to Planned Parenthood!"

"Melissa, the doctors there aren't as well trained as the ones you've been seeing all your life."

"I can't pay. Planned Parenthood is free!"

"Look, you're still underage—"

"I don't have money! I can't ask my parents!"

My pediatrician sighed. "Just have your psychiatrist call me."

I fished another dime out of my pocket and called Dr. Sternbach.

"Oh, *veh!*" he said. "Your doctor, he should call *me!*"

"But, Dr. Sternbach, my pediatrician said you should call *him!*" I tried to give Dr. Sternbach the number.

"Your doctor, *he* should call *me!*" Sternbach yelled, and he hung up.

I felt so scared my stomach hurt. He was angry, which I hadn't expected.

I stood in the phone booth staring down at the mica in the concrete sidewalk. The wind had died down. I could hear him loud and clear.

I dialed my pediatrician again and explained that my analyst insisted I have him make the phone call.

He sighed. "These psychiatrist guys—they're all like that. Give me the number."

On Thursday evening I arrived early for group therapy with butterflies in my stomach. All I could think of was that Dr. Sternbach was angry and that I didn't know why. I sat in his living room, where the group always met. Marcia, the secretary, had just arrived, and I started to tell her that I was worried Dr. Sternbach was mad at me. She looked alarmed. Then Dr. Sternbach came out of his office, but instead of sitting down and waiting for one of us to start talking, he beckoned to me to follow him down the hall to his office. He shut the door and gestured to a seat.

"Explain, please, what you have been doing." He drummed angrily on his armrest.

Even before I started explaining, I realized he was *very* angry. I tried to sit quietly and almost wondered if he might hit me. I told him again that the condom had broken, probably because it was old or because I had been a virgin and did have a hymen, must have, since it hurt when Walt first pushed inside me, and that I already had a Planned Parenthood appointment to find out whether I was pregnant and to take steps if I was, have an abortion, that is. I felt that I was handling the situation fairly well.

Sternbach glowered at me. "Did you not tell your mother?"

At once I felt weak, the wind knocked out of me. I wondered whether he would actually tell my mother, and what I could feel if he did. I still believed he must be right, but I would never find the strength to get through an abortion if I had to confide in my mother. The thought of telling her I was afraid I might be pregnant, of revealing to her that I was counting the minutes and seconds until my next period, chilled me.

"No, I do not want to discuss this with my mother," I said.

"You know, your mother would find this *very* hard to forgive, if you had an abortion and did not tell her."

I began to weep, because I had offended him and he would not forgive me. If I did not agree that my mother was generous, he would tell me I was psychotic. Now I had a problem. Now I had a real problem. If I didn't tell her, he would be mad at me, and if I did tell her, I would not have the strength to go through with the things I needed to do.

I sat there crying as he went on.

"I am very disappointed in you. I have *nothing* against sex, you know that. But this is crazy and careless. And you are oversexed."

He went on for a long time, and I tried to blot out what he was saying as he said it. He told me it was time for the group to begin, and I went in and sat down; everyone expressed concern to see me so upset, and I told my story, and also related how I planned to go to Planned Parenthood and how Walt had been with me every step of the way.

"And she talks about an abortion as if it were nothing!" Dr. Sternbach said.

"Abortions are legal now, and safe," I said. I knew that—the *Roe v. Wade* decision had just been made, and every girl in the school knew. We had all seen the black-and-white photo in *Ms.* magazine of Gerri Santoro, belly down on the floor, her knees drawn up under her armpits, one hand clutching a towel that could not stop the visible bleeding from the amateur abortion gone wrong.

But more than anything, I wanted for him to agree with me, to tell me that if I were pregnant, I would have nothing to worry about. I'd be taken care of.

"How safe is it for you emotionally?" he thundered. "I have treated women who had abortions before. And they always come to me afterward crying, 'I killed the next president of the United States!' They dream about the baby and who it would have been, how it might have developed, for years. They are depressed and need long treatment for depression."

It had never occurred to me that I would feel this way, but I thought he must be right. I felt flattened, as though I were lying under heavy stones. I could hardly breathe through his tirade, and the rest of the group was also silent. Only Hannah, editor at a woman's magazine, spoke up, saying, "Really, Dr. Sternbach, an abortion is just not the dangerous emotional big deal it used to be! Several young women in my office—"

But she got no further.

"This is not true! *You* are hostile," he added, pointing a finger at her, and she, too, fell silent and started to cry. He aimed a final shot at me: "You are the *only* patient whom I have never been able to influence!"

Hannah bowed her head. She was the one of whom I was to grow most fond, since she often stuck up for me and shook her head sympathetically when I told her stories about my mother.

ELEVEN

Oversexed

What's love got to do with it

TERRY BRITTEN AND GRAHAM LYLE

You are oversexed!" Sternbach said in my next session, as I cringed. I hadn't even lain down on the couch when he started talking. I'd gotten my period but wanted to forget my terror. I wanted to talk, to tell him I was scared, to say that I missed Walt even though I did want to break up with him, but I could not keep a train of thought going as he continued to speak in a loud voice.

"Your doctor, he said to me, usually these young girls are luckier than they're worth, but I am telling you, you could have been pregnant! And what would your *mother* have thought? What would your *mother* say? She knows I am treating you."

"Yes, but I don't want to tell her about my life."

"I trusted you to behave more sensibly than you have! What you have done here is absolutely crazy! Crazy!"

I felt guilty and worthless. When I left his office, I walked toward Broadway in a daze, not quite remembering what he had said, knowing there was something terribly wrong with me.

Maybe I had told him that I wanted to kiss a boy. Maybe I had actually kissed one, or maybe I had described the way Walt made love. In analysis, Dr. Sternbach constantly reminded me, you're required to say everything that comes to mind. My longing for a boyfriend whom I could love came to mind a great deal. Regrets for sleeping with Walt never came to mind, although I realized that Sternbach expected me to have them.

Because Sternbach said I was crazy, because crazy meant "oversexed," I wanted to get well, so I observed and documented every tiny surge in sexual feeling in my journal and in my session. If I told him about these moments, he could cure me. To my journal, I confessed my desire to look at Walt's penis and touch it, my fond memories of having done so, and my amusement at recollections of Walt ejaculating into his cat's face, the cat slurping semen off its whiskers with a look of ecstasy. There's a melancholy tone in those old journals—I knew the cat was having a better time than I was, but still I missed Walt, confessing that more to my journal than to Sternbach, though I felt compelled to tell him the truth even when he showed open disgust. Most of my good times with Walt had occurred before I lost my virginity. He cuddled me, we touched and kissed, and his cat got sprayed in the face.

"*Ach*! You have no interests," said Sternbach. "You are only interested in sex! And you want this crazy boy who takes heroin because your father is an alcoholic and your brother is smoking pot!"

My father was an alcoholic, although not according to Dr. Berkeley, and my brother smoked pot. But Walt wasn't just a boy who had used heroin. He was smart, well read, and sexy. He wrote well.

"Do you want a boyfriend who is a drug addict?" Dr. Sternbach had asked angrily.

"No, of course not," I had said. But I did miss Walt—the sight of him, his house, his plants, his bedroom, his hand holding mine, his living room in which, once, his father served me, his sister, and Walt pancakes on blue plates. Dr. Sternbach seemed not to want me to talk about any of Walt's interests or qualities. I didn't want to see Walt as all bad.

In my first month or two on Sternbach's couch, he'd never yelled. I remembered him gently pointing out the mittens I had forgotten on his chair and how glad I had been to see them again—they were favorites.

During these quiet moments on the couch, I remembered a witch mask I'd made at summer camp, how I'd gone to the crafts teacher and said, "I want to make something ugly," and how the result—a papier-mâché hag with a hairy wart—became my Halloween costume that year. I looked around the room again and again: the grotesque, snarling Hindu mask on the back of the door seemed to be growling just what I was feeling: "Look how ugly I am! Watch me being ugly or loud!"

In the wake of my breakup with Walt, I worked harder than ever in Felicia's class. One day, as Mom and I were taking off our coats in the foyer, Felicia beckoned to me to come into the studio. Mom's eyebrows questioned; she looked around like a guinea pig hoping for a carrot.

"Celine, I'm just going to borrow your daughter for a minute," Felicia said.

When I walked in, Felicia looked so serious that I thought she was going to tell me I was doing everything wrong or was not good enough for the class and should leave.

"Look," she said, measuring her words. "You need a *real* ballet class, dear. This is a class for ladies—and you're very welcome to stay, and I hope you continue. But you need more than this." She shrugged, looked me in the eye. I felt a rush of enormous relief.

She put on reading glasses and glanced at a piece of paper in her hand. "Now, I've written down the address of Finis Jhung's ballet school for you—I've already asked them to send you a schedule. You really should go there, and if you're serious about this, pretty much at least five days a week." The next afternoon, I went to Finis's ballet studio on 72nd Street, right above a bakery with gorgeous, gooey cakes in the window.

As I emerged from the dressing room into the studio, the intermediate class dancers were zooming across the floor in grand jetés, and when they'd all finished, Finis put them back in rows for short, slow stretches, a "reverence," he said, to slow, calm music. The class finished and everyone clapped. Finis sat on a stool and sipped tea as the adult advanced beginners—that was me—wandered onto the cracked linoleum studio floor.

"Turrrrn those thighs out!" Finis crooned as he led us through a series of tendus before putting us at the barre.

I wanted for Dr. Sternbach to understand that I'd found something wonderful in dance. He waved his hand in disgust.

"Dance is for you only a substitute for sex," he said. "Because you have no orgasm."

He had a point. I had no orgasm. *That,* he insisted, was one reason I was "oversexed." But I loved standing at the barre feeling myself getting stronger; I loved the music; I loved being able to move across the floor with my arms and legs coordinated. I wanted to tell him, but he started speaking.

"*Ach,* when I was young, I had three girlfriends, and I could go a long time. One of them, she wanted me to keep going, and I did, and then she would want to fuck again and again. A nymphomaniac. She had no orgasm. Otherwise she would have felt satisfied instead of wanting to go and go and go." He coughed, and even the cough sounded angry.

I was to hear a great deal about Sternbach's love life. I was to hear that in a theater in Vienna, a woman beside him reached out in the dark and grabbed his penis. He tried to reach into her lap, too, and she pushed his hand away. I was to hear that when a man "gives" a woman an orgasm, she is "so grateful," and he was talking about his wife. I was to learn that when he'd left his first wife, she sent long, enraged letters to him, "like a Medea," he'd said, laughing. But now he, his first wife, and his second all sat down to dinner together weekly. I believed him when he said they were the best of friends. He told me that before the war, the woman he truly loved, a pharmacologist injured in a workplace accident, on whom he cheated while she was recovering in the hospital, slapped him across the face when she ran into him with another woman. If it had not been for the war, he was certain she would have wanted him back. After the war, when she was married to someone she did not love and had settled in Australia, she said she'd had the best time in her life with Sternbach and sent her granddaughter off to visit him in New York. Listening to all this, I thought he had a family he had put back together after his terrible losses, and I felt lucky, with the rest of the group, to be, in a way, a part of it.

"Sex," Sternbach repeated in the next session, "is forbidden to you because of your father. Because he touched you. Dance is nothing for you. You just want to dance because you have no orgasm." I knew this could not be true, but I didn't know how to say so without incurring anger. Maybe he did not understand, maybe he didn't mean exactly what he said but wanted me to be more aware of sex.

I thought of Dad, drunk and weepy in my bedroom by night, slapping me by day. As if he could read my mind, Sternbach said, "You feel guilty because of what your father did, because you seduced him."

This made me sweat with guilt. I had glimmers of remembering that I wanted my father to come into my room, even though what he did made me feel guilty and confused. I told Sternbach I'd once taken off my pajama bottoms and lain there pretending to be asleep, and on that occasion my father had found them around my ankles, pulled them up around my waist, and left the room without touching me. Only when I seemed very sleepy or unconscious did he touch me.

"You should not feel guilty," Sternbach said, "because you were too young to feel inhibited. You were only a little girl."

I *had* seduced Dad, Sternbach said, but I was *not* to blame.

I blamed myself anyway.

I struggled in a number of sessions to tell Sternbach how much I wanted to dance, how a dance class, and the performances I dreamed of, allowed me to express love and hatred and humor and delight with my arms, my legs, my feet, my whole body. While I was moving to music, I could forget myself. I loved the challenge of the demanding exercises, and I loved the way my body was changing, my back straightening, my legs strengthening, my arms growing leaner, elegant. I loved working at the same exercises with all the other students, feeling united in the common goal of learning together. The class became a family. I loved the daily rituals of stretching, chatting, clapping in appreciation of the teacher at the end of class. I started taking two classes a day—I'd lie down or do homework in the dressing room between them.

Sex was forbidden to me by my unconscious, Dr. Sternbach said, but I knew that any mention of sexual feeling when I met boys would be criticized. Did I rub my clitoris? Sometimes I told him I was tired, sometimes I told him my hands were cold.

"So put them under hot water!" he yelled. I knew there was something wrong with me, because when I talked about masturbation with my best friend, she said, "You mean you never just kind of feel around down there?"

I was still calorie counting and vomiting, another habit Sternbach deemed a substitute for sex and which he told me to stop doing. I wanted to lose a few pounds; I ate frantically whenever I heard my parents fighting, and then vomited. Another friend tried to comfort me.

"Oh, you'll have an orgasm," she said. "It's not always that great. It's like a coin turning over."

One day Sternbach said he wouldn't see me or talk to me until I stopped calorie counting and vomiting. Eating and vomiting had been another escape, like going to his office, and I did not want to lose both, so I did stop vomiting. I gained some weight, but I felt that because I'd given up the bingeing and purging, I had a right to the ballet and African dance.

Sternbach wanted me to talk about sex or my sexual fantasies. I wanted to talk about how, after weeks and months of ballet, after trying very hard to stand straight, turn out my thighs, point my foot in front with my heel turned out, all the while feeling as though my foot were a clunky block of wood, one day, I succeeded. One day, my foot didn't feel like a block of wood. One day, I could feel my toes reaching and the muscular pull on the arch of my foot when I pointed it. I looked down and saw the shape of my pointed foot and I realized all those classes had paid off. I could hold my turn-out. I could do a plié. I could move. I started trying different studios, different teachers. I came to sessions filled with news about what I'd danced and "now I can do sixteen changements" and, ultimately, "I am going to be a dancer."

"You are not a dancer!" he yelled. "You are a dance *student,* that's all." Phlegm burbled in his throat as he said it.

"I started dance class with my mother, Dr. Sternbach," I said, hoping he would approve because he wanted me to get along with her.

"*Ach!* She probably lets you think you are a dancer. You are not. How is your mother?"

I lay on the couch wondering whether I should tell the truth, feeling I must.

"Well?" he asked.

"Mom and I were walking home together yesterday. The bookstore had put up a poster in the window of Santa Claus with a naked lady on his lap. It was funny."

"So *you* would like to have been that naked lady!" He glared. "Yes, I can see you just wanted to be the naked lady on the lap of Santa Claus. *Right?*"

"No, no, I wouldn't." I felt desperate. Did I? Was he right? I hadn't thought that way at all. But maybe I was wrong? "It was just a funny poster. When Mom saw the Santa Claus poster, she got angry. She went into the bookstore to tell the man to take it down because it was confusing to children. I didn't stay. I went ahead of her, home."

"You have no consideration for her." He arched his eyebrows, as if to say he saw right through me. "You could have waited for her. You are mean to her."

"But she's—there's something wrong. She's very childish."

"So what?" he yelled. "So she's childish! My God! Have a little understanding for her! It's amazing that she hasn't killed herself, with her marriage."

I was bent on continuing dance, though it began to feel like something illicit. I'd go to class but not mention it to Sternbach, and since I felt guilty, I wouldn't look Finis, my dance teacher, in the eye. I had sort of a crush on Finis by that time, and instead of smiling and thanking him whenever he gave me a correction, I stared straight ahead. I must have seemed either extremely rude or crazy—paralyzed as I was by fear.

I loved the shabbily genteel ballet studio with the peeling linoleum, the aromas of cakes and powdered sugar and cream confections floating up from below. Once, as I extended my foot in a tendu, a cockroach emerged from the water pipe leading to the bakery and scuttled past, missing the jabbing movement of my foot by a hair. But everything was beautiful at the ballet. If Mom and Dad were fighting, I noticed it less and less. I had my home away from home, the ballet studio, and I could go there at least six days a week.

Watching Judith Jamison dance *Cry*, which Ailey had choreographed for her, filled me with a joy and longing that I knew I had been missing all my life, I told Sternbach. I had what some might call a religious experience watching Jamison dance. I knew that if I could see movement like that, hear music like that, attempt to learn to approximate movement like that myself, I'd never think of killing myself again.

I tried to explain the experience of watching her dance—I spoke of Jamison's height, her rippling arm movements, the proud movements of her head, all the subtleties that made for grandeur on the stage. I described the music—Laura Nyro and Alice Coltrane, the choral, passionate "Right on! Be free!" lyrics—until my throat swelled with emotion so that I could hardly get out any words. I had a picture in my mind of Jamison moving ecstatically onstage, her arms raised, the music pounding, her face filled with light, her torso rolling. Sternbach broke into my rapture.

"She is free, you think."

"Yes," I agreed, hearing his sarcasm, knowing I was dooming myself to at least ten minutes of lecture on my illusions. I should be realistic; I should understand that dancers work hard, very hard, that there is nothing free about dance, and anyway, you are only a student, you are not a dancer.

I wanted to tell him that Jamison expressed everything I was feeling but unable to say. *Cry* seemed to mirror my own yearning, my own painful, patient longing. I felt solitude, strength, sorrow, and Jamison danced these feelings. I went to see Jamison dance night after night, and the sight of her whirling, her arms flung up in hope and sadness, stirred in me a completely new sense of what it was possible to express.

"Give this up! You are not a dancer!" Dr. Sternbach insisted in every session when I mentioned dance. "What happens when you masturbate? Can you tell me, please?"

What happened was I lay on my bed wishing my room had a lock. What happened was my mind went blank. What happened was my hands felt cold—

"You want for me to beat you," he said. "Your father beat you, and this is what you want!"

The words thudded into me. Dad had hit me, slapped me. I vaguely remembered a world I had invented in kindergarten that I called "the spanking machine." I daydreamed that children had to slide down a series of mazelike chutes and be paddled by some mechanism—the contraption in my fantasy might have been invented by Rube Goldberg. I vaguely remembered liking this fantasy as a small child. I didn't like it now, but it seemed familiar.

"Maybe you would like for me to spank you?" Dr. Sternbach said coaxingly as I lay on the couch.

I started to cry.

"Even if it would help you?" he asked in sympathetic tones.

"I don't want that." But I could now not push the image of him spanking me out of my head.

TWELVE

Closer to Mom

A mother's love is very touching, of course,
but it is often curiously selfish.

OSCAR WILDE, *A Woman of No Importance*

Soon after my scolding for the condom break with Walt, Dr.
Sternbach emerged from his office with a smile and beckoned
me to come right in. He gestured toward the chair, not the couch,
so I figured he had something particular to say.

"I have decided it would be good for your mother to come here
with you so you can get closer to her. What do you think about that?"

I felt sad. I felt like I had to do this, because otherwise I would
never develop any real relationships.

"Mom has her own psychoanalyst, right? She still goes to
Aunt Berkeley, I think."

"That is not the point. You are now fifteen years old, and
you have a bad relationship with her. I think there is hope for a
good one. Your father is crazy—he is schizophrenic, and I do
not think he can develop relationships. But your mother tries
very hard, and she loves you very much."

Mom loved me? Very much? I so wanted this to be true, and
Dr. Sternbach seemed absolutely to believe it.

"Do you think my mother could change? I mean, become
someone I could talk to?"

Sternbach leaned forward in his La-Z-Boy, his eyebrows rising. "You are *so* narcissistic. Do you know how many people come to analysis and want their wife to change? Or their husband? Or their *boyfriend*?" He gave me a look, pointing his finger at me. "*You* are the only person whom you can change! It is *you* who have to change, not your mother." If he were right, and I wrong in thinking she did not care about me, then I must be very bad. Nothing. Just a self-centered, empty person, as he said.

"Yes, I see," I said. "But she's strange. I just never know what she'll do—"

"So she's a little strange! You are a terrible daughter," Dr. Sternbach said. "So adolescent! Your dependence on her makes you hate her! I knew a schizophrenic who told his mother, 'Don't you know that I hate you so much because I need you so much?' You need your mother. She gives you everything. That is why you resent her."

I didn't know what to say. I knew she was paying for my expensive girl's school and for my analysis and had paid for my summer camps and dance classes. She bought the food. I knew Dad did not make enough money with his teaching job. I knew my mother wanted my love very much. I remembered her grief when Gaga died.

I had arrived home from fourth grade to see my mother collapsed on Dad's shoulder, in tears. I heard her muffled sobs before I saw her—the two of them were pressed against a wall near the window in Dad's music room, almost hidden by a piano and by Dad's huge rubber tree and ferns. They looked almost as if they were cuddling. Mom was shaking and Dad was holding her, the expression on his face confused, patting her back. His arms were gripping her, her knees almost buckling, and on his desk, the phone was lying off the hook.

I had never seen the two of them in each other's arms like that. I heard Mom sobbing words I didn't understand.

"Oh, she did herself in. She did herself *in*." She groaned. I didn't know the meaning of the phrase and didn't know whom Mom could be talking about.

Standing in the doorway, I dropped my schoolbag. Dad saw me and murmured something to Mom.

Mom stepped away from Dad, her face red, her eyes teary. She turned to me and said, "Melissa, I have some sad news." I followed her into the kitchen.

"It's good we saw Gaga on Saturday," she began in a shaky voice.

"Is Gaga dead?"

Mom sat down at the counter. Her face registered astonishment. "How did you know?" I moved toward her. The kitchen was narrow. It would have been awkward for her to get up and edge around me, but she was looking past me at the door.

"Well, is she?" I asked again, sure the answer must be yes, but wondering why.

"She had a heart attack on Sunday morning," Mom said. "Aunt Gwen just phoned."

I wondered if Dad had hung up the phone in his music room.

"Aunt Gwen phoned Gaga, but no one answered."

"Why did no one answer?"

"Gwen had keys to the house and went in and found Gaga in bed, looking as though she were asleep," Mom said dully.

I thought of Gaga, her pink paisley scarf billowing prettily. "Hi-ho, dearie!" she would cry, waves of Shalimar enveloping anyone standing near. Whenever we visited her home in Old Greenwich, I would lift the stopper from that perfume bottle and sniff. One whiff almost made you drunk. A deep, poisonous green, the color of absinthe, it has stayed with me as a holy grail of aromas. To this day, I sniff random perfume bottles, hoping, whenever I come across some vintage oriental Emeraude by Coty cologne, to find the fragrance that, to me, defined Gaga. I miss her now, and I missed her then. But whenever I mentioned Gaga, my mother grew crisp and overly cheerful. Something felt off, but by then I had learned from Dr. Sternbach that feelings were usually misleading.

"Your mother," Dr. Sternbach said, "your mother has had a difficult life."

"I guess so," I said, thinking of her groans that day and her odd cheer ever since. "I know Mom had had a terrible relationship with her mother," I said. "She never wanted Gaga to come visit or for us to go to see her."

"You see?" He nodded at me. "Don't you want to break the chain?" I was afraid to contradict him.

Whatever Mom did, she meant well, Sternbach insisted. I should not snap at her or complain to her, he said. She loved me. My problem lay in not understanding how giving she was. Because Dr. Sternbach told me these things, I knew he must be right. He was adjusting the height of the La-Z-Boy and fiddling with the cord on his phone, which had gotten tangled with some papers. As he tried to remove them, the phone fell down, and I picked it up and handed it to him.

"*Mein Gott!*" he yelled, looking at me. I felt, for a moment, as if the accident of the phone falling was my fault, or that he blamed me, and I sat quietly.

"So, next Wednesday, you will come with your mother?"

I wasn't sure. He sat looking at me, tapping his foot. He shook his head.

"You think you are so great! So exceptional. But really, you are *average*. Just ordinary. Nothing exceptional at all. A girl within the range of a normal IQ, that's all."

"Yes, you told me."

"Your mother probably encourages your idea that you are special. She has her own problems. So, we will set this up?"

Mom arrived before me for our session together. I had come from school, she from our Upper West Side apartment. By the time I arrived, she was roaming around the waiting room peering at Dr. Sternbach's art, running her fingers over the frames, adjusting the paintings on the walls, and leaning over his sculptures, brushing dust off them. She shook her head at the George Grosz drawing of tough-faced men wielding cigars. Scratches and tattoos adorned their bodies, sneers their faces. A busty barmaid leered at the men.

Mom turned to something that seemed to appeal to her more—a Viennese statue of an angel. She grabbed the pedestal, as if she were going to move the angel toward her. I was about to tell her to move away from it. It always amazed me that she behaved as though she didn't know she shouldn't touch other people's things. I could imagine her accidentally breaking something.

Dr. Sternbach walked into the room, and Mom whirled around, knocking the angel slightly so that it swayed behind her. She held out her arms to Dr. Sternbach as if greeting a long-lost friend. Her pink tam slipped sideways, falling off her head. She left the hat on the floor as she opened her arms wider, rearing back with apparent anticipation, and called, "What ho? What *ho?*" As she did so, I cringed with embarrassment, telling myself that she meant well.

Before Dr. Sternbach had gotten past the first syllable in "hello," my mother was hugging him. Red-faced, he wrapped his arm around her for a second, then stepped back.

"Well, Mrs. Knox," he said, "you seem in a good mood."

"Yes!" Mom said. "And you *certainly* have some *interesting* art!" Pronouncing the word "interesting" in such a way that it suggested "revolting," she eyeballed his George Grosz drawing again with a scowl.

"Perhaps you prefer a different kind of art?" He smiled at her. He seemed genuinely to enjoy her company. More than mine? I stood shifting from foot to foot a few feet away from them. Just as I was wondering if we would spend the whole session out here in the waiting room chatting about his art, he gestured for her to come into his office.

She'd forgotten about her hat, which remained lying on his parquet floor. I picked it up and handed it to her.

"Oh, yes!" she said, flashing me a wide smile, and brushed past me into his office.

He had set up two upholstered side chairs right in front of his La-Z-Boy. Mom settled herself in the one near the window and gestured me toward the other chair as if she were a maître d.' I sat and crossed my legs. She leaned over, patted me on the knee, put her face next to mine, and said, "Did you have a good day in school, dearie?" She was uncomfortably close to my face, her hand now patting my thigh. I moved back. She sat back in her own seat, a slightly hurt expression on her face.

"So your mother is asking how you *are!*" Sternbach said. "She is *interested!* She wants to know! She really would *like* to know how you are feeling." He gripped his armrest and smiled at Mom.

She flashed a grin at him, turned again to me, looking me up and down. "You look a bit depressed, dearie. Are you depressed?"

I hadn't been, until she started patting me. "It's just school," I said.

"I wonder if you're thinking of applying to free schools—this was *always* the time of year you did that—I wonder if you're replaying that old record again." She gazed at me as if wanting me to admit this.

"School is fine," I said, "just *somewhat* depressing sometimes."

"Well, but this time of year is *always* when you want to leave school, isn't it?" Mom gave me a pert look, as if going over well-traveled ground. "You were *always* talking about Summerhill and A. S. Neill and some upstate free school like that this time last year. *Right?*" She was speaking to Dr. Sternbach, smiling archly at him—like a student looking for high marks from a teacher.

"There's a lot of work in school, Mom."

"But maybe not *all* work?" Sternbach gazed at me conspiratorially. "You have yourself some fun, right?"

There was one boy I liked, Howie, he of the stairwell kisses. And although his kisses didn't live up to my idea of romance, and were not as good as Walt's had been, he looked handsome in the half-light. Howie had invited me to meet him for coffee at the Chock Full o'Nuts on 86th and Lexington.

"I have some friends," I said. Mom and Dr. Sternbach were looking at me expectantly.

"Is it possible you even have a date?" asked Dr. Sternbach. Mom looked from me to Dr. Sternbach. Her lips twitched. I told her I was meeting my friend Howie for coffee on Saturday afternoon. The expression on her face suggested one cup of coffee would lead straight to pregnancy.

"Do you know this person well?" Mom asked. "How long have you known him? Did someone you know well introduce you?" I could answer every question, but I knew she would need for me to answer more.

"Mom," I said, realizing I must sound peevish, "he's just a nice person I met at the class dance, and we are going to have coffee."

"I thought you were still seeing *that Walt*," she said, narrowing her eyes. I hadn't seen *that Walt* for a few weeks, as she must have known.

"No, I'm not."

Mom pursed her lips. "Well, I hope you'll be *very* careful," she said and nodded at Dr. Sternbach, as if cueing him to speak.

"I am not against sex!" Sternbach said, speaking in Mom's direction. Then he smiled in mine, as though he and I shared a secret. I had told him about kissing Howie at the school dance. Mom knew nothing about the pregnancy scare I'd endured with Walt, or Dr. Sternbach's reaction to that event.

Mom and I sat in those chairs in front of him like children in front of the kindergarten teacher. I felt she would never dare contradict a psychoanalyst, so that I'd be allowed out to Chock Full o'Nuts. Dr. Sternbach turned to her again.

"Mrs. Knox, I think things are going well with Melissa. Her grades are improving, and she seems to be coming out of the shell, as you say, right?"

Mom tossed her head, seeming to consider. "*Hmmmm,*" she said. She looked around the room, drummed her fingers on the armrests of her chair. She turned to me. "Yes, dearie, I think you are feeling a bit better, aren't you?" Her eyes looked desperate, but I believed she meant to be happy. Mom leaned back in her seat and sighed, pointing and flexing her feet as if she were in ballet class. She stole glances at Dr. Sternbach, as if hoping he'd notice her feet. I looked away, toward the African masks on the bookcase.

"Tell me, Mrs. Knox, have *you* always been this depressed?" My gaze snapped back, Sternbach leaning toward Mom. First her eyes went wide, as if he'd just said the most absurd, outrageous, insulting thing she'd ever heard in her entire life. Then she caved in. I saw a tear slide down her cheek.

"What? How did you know?" Surreptitiously, she glanced at me.

"Melissa, will you sit in the waiting room for a moment?" he asked. I left the room. The white noise machine was on, and I couldn't hear their voices, so I tiptoed to his office door, leaned my ear against it, and listened.

"—nothing is going to change," Sternbach was saying.

"Yes, well," Mom sobbed, "that's very helpful." Silence.

I padded back to the waiting room, barely making it to a chair before Sternbach came out. "Would you please come back in?"

I returned and sat back down. Mom had clearly been crying but looked calmer.

Dr. Sternbach didn't ask any more questions, and after a few minutes of silence, he glanced at his watch and told us it was time to go.

"Well, you're growing up!" Mom said to me on the bus home. "Hmmm. A date for coffee with a boy!" She looked at me expectantly. I knew she wanted me to tell her more, but I couldn't bring myself to do so. Still, I wanted to please Dr. Sternbach. I wanted to have a good life.

"So you and Walt aren't together at *all* anymore?" Mom asked. "That must be *sad*." Mom's face had the look of a woman watching a soap opera in which the bad guy is about to get destroyed. I didn't see any sadness in her face. I didn't want to talk about Walt, and I knew exactly how to distract Mom.

"You met Dad at Aunt Berkeley's, didn't you, Mom?"

"Oh, yes!" she said. "I didn't know any men at all, and Aunt Berkeley was like a fairy godmother introducing us. I had no idea what was the matter with me!"

Her voice a little too loud, her giggle high and piercing, Mom told me about the time she'd noticed a "strange smell" from "down there." I was really glad we were back on Broadway where no one could hear us when that story came out. Concerned that she was suffering from a dread disease, she went to her gynecologist, who pulled out a tampon that had lain ripening for several weeks.

"Isn't that funny?" she prodded. I was not laughing. I was staring straight ahead, hoping to get home before running into anyone we knew.

"How old were you when your gynecologist found that tampon?" I asked.

"Oh, around thirty."

For Mom's birthday that year, I gave her a copy of Erica Jong's *Fear of Flying,* then a best seller, which Dr. Sternbach had dismissed with a wave of his hand and the following comment, in his heavily Viennese-accented English: "Jong writes well of her fucking."

I wouldn't be surprised to learn that I'd been the only one to hear about my mother's festering tampon. I'd bet she never told Dr. Berkeley.

THIRTEEN

By the Sea

By the sea, by the sea, by the beautiful sea,
You and I, you and I, oh! How happy we'll be.

HAROLD ATTERIDGE, "By the Beautiful Sea"

When my cousin Ceci, her family back from England for summer vacation, called to ask if I might come to the shore for the weekend, I was thrilled. Walt and I had been broken up for a few months, and I still thought about him every day and remembered things like the smell of the back of his neck. I needed to get away.

My mother was hovering nearby as I spoke on the kitchen phone. Ceci added, tonelessly, unenthusiastically, that her mum would like to invite mine. "The sisters!" she whispered.

My stomach contracted at the thought of Mom diving off the dock with my cousins and me. When she'd come to a swimming hole on parents' visiting day at summer camp, she'd made comments about my first two-piece bathing suit. "Maybe you'll catch a fish in your bra!" I didn't want her to come to the shore with me. I didn't mention my cousin's invitation—and I felt sure Ceci wouldn't mind.

As Ceci and I spoke, Mom was humming around the kitchen loudly, her ears trained in the direction of my call. I shot her a glance, and she did go silent. In my head, I could hear Dr. Stern-bach telling me I should not be mean to her.

"Dad's not here, thank God, so we can relax," Ceci was saying.

"I hate that fucking bastard!" said Grace, who had picked up the extension on their end.

"You wouldn't say that if Mum were in the house," Ceci laughed. Grace hung up.

"So you're coming down, then, OK?" said Ceci. I could see her teasing look, and I imagined all my cousins crowding the living room with laughs and ice cream. Plus, I wanted to find out why they hated their dad as much as I hated mine.

"How about every weekend?" I said.

Ceci giggled. "How about bringing some beer?"

"OK!" Walt and I hadn't drunk beer. We'd shared a joint once. High, I couldn't stop laughing, but when I was crossing the street, trying to go from the Cathedral of Saint John the Divine to the Hungarian Pastry Shop, I had to look down, because I thought my body stopped at the waist and I was just gliding along. When I saw my feet walking, I knew they must really be there.

"I'm kidding!" Ceci was saying. "You don't have to bring beer. We'll get that here."

"I can bake chocolate chip cookies. Besides, I like to cook."

"I remember your cookies. Make lots. Maybe we can get Grace to eat. Or Ginny. They're always dieting."

I boarded the Greyhound bus with a huge container of Toll House chocolate chip cookies. All the way down to the shore, I stared out the window thinking about the way I'd dumped Walt—on the phone. Because I knew I'd never manage to do it in person.

"You're doing this because your shrink told you to?" he'd asked.

"I wouldn't have done it if I hadn't at least partially agreed with him," I replied. He called me back later, and I told him he was taking the news a lot better than I would have in his position. He said, "You think I'm taking this well? . . . You're putting me very close to the edge of something. All I can say is good-bye. Good-bye!" and he hung up. His good-bye had been ringing in my ears ever since. Whenever I told Dr. Sternbach that despite Walt's drug problem, I felt I'd really gotten something out of the relationship, that I missed some things Walt and I had done together, he shook his head angrily and said, "Psychotic."

Aunt Gwen met me at the bus station in a white bathing suit that offset her rosy, sun-soaked look. I offered her the cookies as soon as I stepped off the bus. She took just one, saying, "Oh, how nice!" Then she passed them back to me.

"Lovey, don't *you* want more? I can get you some milk to have with the cookies when we're home." On her face was the longing of a child to be fed, to be loved. She often didn't deliver whatever she offered—she was known for entering rooms mumbling offers of tea and then disappearing into the kitchen for hours, forgetting all about boiling water or finding teabags. But she seemed to me to mean well.

The cousins were still down on the beach when we arrived, so I sat with Aunt Gwen on their back porch, listening to the peaceful clinking of a bit of metal against a pole, the subdued calling of seagulls, hums of planes and small craft, the gentle wash of waves against the dock pilings. Heron cries, long, like the cry of a loon, came occasionally. I watched the late afternoon sun, looking forward to the vivid orange and purple sunsets for which their stretch of shoreline was known. Aunt Gwen was beside me, asking, every few minutes, no matter how often I said no, "Wouldn't you like a slice of cake, lovey? Are you sure not?" Her preoccupied state was so typical I hardly noticed, although there seemed a sadder than usual mood to her continual chatter.

"We're all on our own this year, lovey, you know, Rob's stayed back in England to work on the house?"

Aunt Gwen had a way of making statements sound like questions. An involuntary whimper—*hmmf?*—a lonely sound, followed each statement.

I passed her the box of chocolate chip cookies. "Would you like one?" She answered, "Yes, thanks, hmmf?" as if she were about to burst into tears.

She took a bite. "It's nice you're here. Oh, sometimes I'm tired with six children? Hmmf?"

I was wondering how to respond when the screen door banged open and slammed shut, feet thudded across the floor, and the loud, giggly voices of my cousins greeted me.

"We were going to come with Mum to pick you up!" Tim shouted.

"But then you fell asleep at the beach, stupid," said Ceci, smiling.

"Well, you twit, that was, of course, your fault," Tim said. They stuck tongues out at each other, laughed, and threw their towels and beach bags on the floor. How I adored my lively cousins. After hugs all around, I offered them cookies, and Tim took a handful.

"Oh, wait 'til after dinner," Ceci scolded. "Let's hit the beach!"

We piled in the car and headed toward the water—Ceci driving. As soon as we were out of Aunt Gwen's earshot, she asked drily, "Aunt Silly's not joining us, I gather?"

Celine—Mom, that is—was indeed not joining us, I assured them.

"Your name captures her character," I said. Tim popped a Coke open and turned to Ceci. "Speaking of silly, what did Mum say at the Chinese restaurant the other night?"

Ceci snickered so loudly I wondered if she would still be able to drive. "We were all sitting around the table, right, and the Chinese waiter comes and passes out the menus. Just as we open them, Mum says—too loud, you know, she's hard of hearing—'Let's have a little food and fill in the chinks.' I died. I swear, I could *not* believe it."

"The waiter heard?"

"We're hoping he didn't speak English," Grace returned.

After a dip in the warm, crashing breakers, we lay around on our towels. Even as the sun set, the weather stayed warm.

"Well, Dad's really angry that we've all come here without him," Ceci confided, "but we told Mum we needed a break." Her voice had gotten more clipped—more English—than when we were little girls playing at Gaga's house. I'd seen them over the years, but on such short trips that we'd never had much time together.

"He hates Americans," said Grace, who had the most English accent of all of them. As the popsicle-orange sun slid lower on the horizon, we started to pack up. "She waits on the bastard hand and foot."

"He's drunk all the time now," Ginny offered. "And, like, he'd *said* he'd never drink if he could leave the States." She looked as though she'd wanted to believe him.

"My father is drunk every night, too," I said. "Throws things. Red in the face."

"It figures," Ginny said. "Two teetotaling sisters marrying two alcoholics, right?"

"Mum would never let us talk about him," Tim said. "She had, like, a rule we could not discuss Dad. So everyone just went to their rooms, skulked alone, waiting for the drunks in the front hall to go home."

Later that evening, I saw Ginny's diary, which she'd left lying open in the room where I was sleeping. She'd written, "I hate that fucking bastard!!!" on page after page. She'd also detailed her father's naked romp through the snow "when there were children present" on January 1.

"Mum's talked to a lawyer who told her to take notes, keep track," Ginny said. "But Mum's afraid he'll get violent."

"Which he obviously won't," Ceci said. "He's too pissed to do anything but piss."

"But she wants to be fair to him," said Tim, who looked as if he understood her longing.

"He's not worked for decades," Ceci said. "She's supporting *him*. He doesn't have a legal leg to stand on."

Back at the house, a wonderful aroma of garlicky sauce hit us as we came up the steps. Aunt Gwen had prepared spaghetti and scallops. She placed an enormous pot of red spaghetti sauce on the table, asked who wanted what to drink, and fluttered back into the kitchen.

"She'll never remember, you know," Tim said. "Might as well get your own drink."

We chattered on about Gwen seeming as distracted as my mother. Ceci shrugged, muttering something about her mum feeling guilty ever since Gaga's death.

"Guilty?" I asked. I stopped eating for a moment, although I was very hungry. Something familiar was coming back, a feeling of confusion. Why guilty?

I forked up a scallop or two and looked around for the bottle of Chianti that I'd seen earlier.

Ceci looked at me. "Didn't you know?"

That familiar feeling intensified, an unfinished-business sort of a feeling. I'd known something was off in the way Mom told the story.

I glanced at Ceci. "My mother said Gaga had died of a heart attack."

Ceci sipped at her wine and looked toward the kitchen. Aunt Gwen was humming vaguely and doing something with pots on the stove.

"What do you *mean*?" I said. "What *really* happened? Please tell me."

Lowering her voice, Ceci said, "Mum drove us to Gaga's, then told us to wait in the car." She rolled her eyes. "I knew something was up. We *never* waited—we came right in."

"But please, *how* did she die?" I asked. I looked over at Aunt Gwen, still bustling around, folding brown paper shopping bags in the kitchen, still apparently not within earshot. I had a feeling I knew the answer to my own question, but I wanted to be told.

Ceci cast me a skeptical look. "Why would Gaga have been sleeping? That made no sense. We were going to her house while she was sleeping? So Grace and I got out of the car and went upstairs," Ceci said.

"Did your Mom see you?"

"No, we snuck in—we were going to wait, but we heard Mom cry out and ran upstairs."

"What did you see?"

"Mum cried out. Then she slammed Gaga's bedroom door and yelled at us not to come in. She was crying."

They waited there, breathless, leaning against the door, listening to their mother sobbing.

"What happened?" I asked.

Gaga, dressed to the nines, her pearls around her neck, her lipstick perfectly applied, her nails neatly manicured, had been found on top of her meticulously made pink-quilted bedspread by Aunt Gwen. A bouquet of roses bloomed in a vase on the nightstand, next to the empty bottle of Seconal. Notes folded like little flowers lay all around her.

I like to think Gaga was wearing her nicest T-straps for her walk into the next world—I like to imagine her arriving in some gorgeous amusement park lit with the colors I remembered flickering from the Palisades across the Hudson. I could see her strolling toward the Ride to Mars, beckoning to all of us: "Come on *over*!"

Why hadn't I ever questioned Mom about the heart attack story? Ceci noticed my surprised expression. For a moment, we stared at each other. Her face reddened slightly; she looked down.

I took a big sip of Chianti.

Ceci looked to the side, as if she might be swallowing a lump. "Gaga left a note for each grandchild."

I thought of Gaga alone in her huge house after Granddad died, his ashes in a copper urn in her bedroom. How we loved visiting, but it was the cousins and the house, the gardens and the beach, the gazebo and the mulberries, not really Gaga whom we knew. We really never spent much time with her. She waved and smiled, passed out presents, showed us photos of herself as a teenage actress in silent films, tied to a railroad track while a bandit in a bandanna throttled her. Lovely kohl-rimmed eyes filled with melodramatic horror stared into the camera with an anguish I had thought entirely mimed.

No, there had never been a heart attack.

Her death had been her finest role? Her perfection?

"She left notes for you and Roland, too," Ceci added.

I felt a weird sense of relief. I wasn't surprised. The heart attack story had never felt right. I hated what Gaga had done, but as always, I admired her style.

Ceci shook her head dismissively. "Grace's note had some tripe—you are a true aristocrat!" My cousin cackled. But she did not remember her own, and may never have seen it, having been only six at the time.

The next morning, a warm bay breeze rifled and salted the curtains. The day was overcast, and we spent a lazy morning drinking coffee and swimming off the dock; I showed Aunt Gwen a few ballet exercises. The house seemed bigger than the last time I'd been there. In the afternoon, Art and I played Monopoly. That evening, he and I sat around talking with Aunt Gwen. Her hand kept working a pen around in a circle as we sat at the supper table, and I kept thinking she was going to cry.

"Tell me, Melissa, how is your *sister* doing? She seems so thin." I knew she meant Mom. Both Mom and Aunt Gwen said "your sister" when they meant "your mother" or "your aunt." We were all used to that.

"Oh, Mom's dieting as usual, but I think she's dealing with things."

"You mean with your dad?"

"Well, I think she ought to divorce him," I said. Aunt Gwen flinched.

"Well . . . she and I have talked, hmmf? But I just think when someone's trying hard, you should go slowly, not rush them, give them credit for *trying.*"

The difference between my mother and her, I realized, was that Aunt Gwen still loved Uncle Rob very much.

"Did Gaga *really* die of a heart attack?"

I was home from the shore, standing in the kitchen with my mother, and I wanted to see whether she would tell the truth if I asked directly.

Mom looked all around the room as if for an exit, pursed her lips, took the kettle off the stove, and poured herself tea. Suddenly, she looked angry.

"Is that something *Gwen* told you?"

"Are you kidding? She's only worried about not hurting anyone's feelings, and trying to keep her kids and Uncle Rob happy." I shook my head, thinking of hunched-over, frantic little Aunt Gwen, whose interest in gossip was absolutely nil.

Mom nodded. "Gwen is always trying to please people. I used to be like that, before analysis. She always wanted to please Dad—I did, too, back then."

I shrugged. "Well, daughters often love their fathers."

Mom's face took on a new look of amazement. "Did *you* love *Dad?*" she asked. Her face begged me to reassure her that I had not.

I felt a wave of embarrassment. "Mom, I'm just—yes, he is my father, and as a small child, I was fond of him. But now please tell me: did Gaga kill herself?"

"How did you *know?*" Her voice rose to a squeak. "Someone must have told you." Her eyebrows receded to her hairline. She looked astonished or enraged, or both.

I shrugged. "Gaga came here and she ate with us and seemed fine—why would she have had a heart attack? Also, you were very upset and Dad was hugging you." I didn't need to say that I'd never seen such a display of affection before.

My mother's face contracted. "Aunt Berkeley thought I shouldn't tell you—she thought it would be better for you if I said Gaga just had a heart attack."

"Mom, I *want* to know."

My mother looked contrite. "Aunt Berkeley didn't want you to be traumatized or anything," she said, and sipped her tea. "Aunt Berkeley was sure it was better to say Gaga had a heart attack."

"I knew you were sad, and I could tell something was wrong."

"I thought I had covered that up! I didn't think you knew I was *sad!*" Mom seemed insulted that I had found her out. My discovery was in bad taste. She grinned and stared with an exaggeration that no one could possibly feel, her eyes boring into me.

"Why did Gaga kill herself?" I asked, leaning toward Mom, whose face fell.

"Oh. Well." She stared off into space. Then she seemed to gather herself, a faint smile appearing on her lips, a ripple running across her brow. Now she looked excited, as if looking forward to a treat that was just out of sight.

"Well, of course, Gwen and the kids were moving to England. That did it."

"What?"

"They were all going away, you see—and Gaga was going to be all alone. Even though Gaga complained to *me* about the mess those kids made—sobbing about the wet bathing suits and the sand all over the floor, she wanted to see them every weekend, and usually did." Mom's eyes glittered with pride that Gaga had confided in her alone, that Aunt Gwen had never known Gaga minded the mess her kids made. Mom had helped Gaga, emptying the lint box on Gaga's dryer, which Gaga had never emptied, but Mom had not let Gaga interfere too much in our family life, the way Gwen had let Gaga interfere.

Mom's foot was tapping and she was stirring her tea, even though there was hardly any tea in the cup and the spoon clinked against the sides of the mug.

"You think Gaga's death is Aunt Gwen's fault?"

Mom leaned against the wall, as if deflated. "No. No, it's not."

"Ceci said Gaga left all the grandchildren notes, personal notes. Where is mine?"

Mom looked away. "There were notes, yes. We read them."

"What about a note for me? I know Grace read her note. I'd like mine."

"No, no," my mother was shaking her head. She put down her cup haphazardly, nearly overturning it.

"Grace's note said she was *a true aristocrat* or something. What did mine say? It was addressed to me—I want to read it."

"I don't remember, but Aunt Berkeley said that none of it was appropriate for children."

"Where is my note now?"

"There wasn't any point in keeping them." Mom shook her head, as if relieved to be rid of the notes.

"It was *mine*! Ceci read Grace's!"

"Well!" My mother shook her head. "Gwen really ought to have known better. None of that was appropriate. Of course, Gwen's never had any help, never had any analysis at all," Mom added with a superior air. "She lacks judgment."

Mom set her tea down and left the kitchen, leaving me swimming in Aunt Berkeley's ideas of what was appropriate.

FOURTEEN

Independence Day

Three cheers for the red, white and blue.

JOHN PHILIP SOUSA, "The Stars and Stripes Forever"

Mrs. Knox, you have been married for twenty-five years. If, during those twenty-five years your husband has not changed—"

My mother nodded, wriggling in her seat as if she couldn't bear the thought of sitting still one more minute.

We were in our mother–daughter session with Dr. Sternbach.

"Why don't you come with me on a vacation to Saint Lucia after my divorce?" Mom turned to me abruptly. Her eyes were wide and pleading. Dr. Sternbach was looking at me.

"Yes, I think that is a good idea," he said. "You two will have a mother–daughter vacation." He smiled. "You can help your mother when she is alone."

"I never *realized* that," Mom told me as we walked home. "Aunt Berkeley never told me Dad wouldn't *change*."

Mom hopped the next plane to Haiti.

Forty-eight lawyer-free hours later, a smiling official awarded her a scroll.

"Is this my divorce?"

Waving away flies, the clerk said, *"Madame, vous êtes libre."*

Mom repeated this line with a smile on her sad face, the day after I flew to meet her, as we breakfasted on a balcony in Soufrière, surrounded by brilliant rain forest greens, neon pinks, and bright yellows, eating soursop and being served coffee by tall, beautiful, young black women who responded to every request with "yes, mistress." One of them asked how old I was. When I said sixteen, her eyes widened. "But where is your husband? Your baby?"

If I'd had any honesty, I might have answered that my baby was sitting right across from me, and my husband, or what passed for one, was probably reclining in his La-Z-Boy yelling at another patient. But I would not have been able to share these insights with anyone, least of all myself.

Back home, Mom boasted that her Haitian divorce papers had "more wax seals than a papal bull!" In a session with Dr. Sternbach a few weeks later, she confided that she'd fallen in love with the gardener at her hotel. She'd gone back to his room with him, adding, "But he had the TV on the whole time."

She blew her nose loudly and talked about how she'd written her gardener many times and he'd never replied. Then he came to visit his grandma in Harlem, and she got to see him.

"That helped," said Mom, sniffling.

Dr. Sternbach gave my mother a sympathetic nod, but while she was wiping off her face with a tissue, he shook his head at me, wagged a finger.

"I ate a big bar of chocolate and felt better," Mom said.

The divorce was old enough to open its eyes and wave its arms around. I thought it would never live to crawl, because Dad was still sleeping on a camp bed in his music room, surrounded by packed boxes. He said he was looking for an apartment. Whenever he left his room, Mom spread apartment listings over his desk. He swept them to the floor.

"I don't want these!" he flung at her.

Eyes wide, voice lilting, she said, "I'm trying to be helpful."

Sometime in June, Mom spread out the apartment listings across Dad's desk as she did almost every day. But this time she gave him a deadline, some three weeks hence: "July 4 must be my Independence Day!" she wrote.

We were all still eating dinner together: Dad, Mom, me, Roland. The evening of the July 4 exhortation, the bread knife found its way into one of Dad's hands, slicing the other badly. Mom fluttered about with ice and bandages. Dad thrust her aside, yelling, "This doesn't hurt! It just may stop my going when you want."

Roland continued to eat in an unhurried fashion.

Mom's note, on violet-ebullient stationery, informed Dad of her find. The apartment was "just down the street."

"You'll find it easy to see the children for dinner and breakfast!" she wrote, placing her missive on his desk blotter.

"But I won't like running into him in the supermarket," she told me.

The night after Dad moved, I heard Mom leap out of bed and open her window, from which you could see Dad's new apartment. "Every time I hear a wino howl, I think your dad is trying to hurt himself," she confessed. She clutched my arm. I told her to shut the window, go back to bed. Her feet were still scuttling around after I went back to my room. I felt her listening, waiting.

When the elevator doors closed over the squeaking wheels of the dolly carting out Dad's final packed box, my brother moved in to his music room. Glass-paned French doors offered little privacy, but Roland covered them with a big brown blanket. Inside his new room, another door led directly to the hall of the building. Roland attempted to hide this door with a Jimi Hendrix poster that could be removed as needed. Mom took to standing outside the French doors, peering in through corners uncovered by the big brown blanket.

I found ways to get her into the kitchen when his girlfriend slipped through the Jimi Hendrix door. One morning, I wasn't fast enough. I heard the glass doors flung open, my mother's shocked voice: "You're too young to be doing *that*!"

Months later, one winter evening, Mom peeked in my brother's door. She beckoned me, loudly whispering, "He's gone completely loco."

Shoving me to the spot free of the blanket, she pointed to flames shooting up from my brother's desk.

She flung open his glass doors, charged in, and put out the fire, and the stench—piles of sweaty socks, unwashed body, stale pot smoke—hit me with full force. Scrawled across Roland's walls were brown letters, announcing UFOs. He'd spilled chocolate milk on his rug weeks before, dipped his finger in it, and written on the walls, "Jesus!" "SHIT!"

"Roland!" she said. "You have to clean up! You have to wash the mess off your wall!"

Roland had fallen asleep with his head on his desk. She shook him awake. "Roland! You have to clean up!"

He turned with a sudden, enraged look, and my mother and I left the room, quickly.

Roland came into the kitchen, looking dazed, the neck of his turtleneck cut out with scissors, a magic-markered image of a flying saucer scrawled across the front.

"What is this you want me to wash off?" he asked loudly. "Should I use Ajax? Are you going to pay me? Where is it, anyway, this thing?" I turned from him. It was late. I had to get up in the morning. I had to go to school. I went to my room and checked to see that my schoolbag was packed, my clean leotards and ballet shoes in my dance bag. I heard Roland yelling and felt afraid, and afraid for Mom. I went back into the kitchen. He had stormed out, and she was sitting at the Formica counter.

"Mom," I said. She was staring straight ahead. "Mom!" I stood in the doorway and then lowered my voice. "Mom, you have to do something, get him a doctor." I felt like my voice was coming from some great distance. I felt as if I were a robot who had been programmed to say what I said. I knew it had to be said but didn't want to be there while the words were being uttered.

"Yes," said my mother, "I will."

She heaved a deep sigh and put her head in her hands.

I'll never forget the Christmas when Roland's door never opened. I knew we had to go visit Dad together—I called Dad and said

I wasn't even sure Roland was home. Dad asked if he should come over, and I said I didn't know.

Roland came in the front door around eleven in the morning, and behind him was a huge street guy who reeked of rum, wore filthy clothes, looked even more stoned.

"I'm Lamar," he giggled. "I'm trust-worth-y." He drew out the word, each syllable extended to the limit. Mom ran out from the kitchen with a tray of coffee and a bowl of Doritos and asked in her perky, little-girl voice whether Roland would like to offer some to his friend.

Lamar disappeared into Roland's room as Roland stood swaying in the hall. I followed Lamar, who was fingering items on Roland's desk.

"Lamar, it's Christmas Day. This is family time. You need to go home now." To my surprise, he followed me out the door to the hallway. His eyes rolled around. I realized that he had no idea where the front door was, so I said, "Just follow me," and he leaned in the direction I'd indicated, swaying on his feet. I took his arm, led him to the still-open front door, waited 'til he was out, and shut it quickly.

Dad arrived around five in the afternoon. Mom had made eggnog. It was strong and had a lot of nutmeg sprinkled on top. Dad sipped it, looked at Mom as if she were the most beautiful woman he had ever seen, and said, "Thank you, darling."

Mom bristled and set down a bowl of nuts she had been going to pass him with a thud so loud that half of them spilled onto the table. Roland sat in a stupor beside Dad, not moving for so long that I had an urge to do something to get him to move. I said, "Let's bring out some more glasses for water." We didn't need water. We didn't need glasses. My voice was all squeaky and artificial. I sounded like Mom. Roland sat there as if he had not heard me. After a long time, he stood up, and just stood and stood and stood. He looked like a waxwork figure; he had less animation than the furniture. My parents sat there, Dad complimenting Mom on the Christmas décor, Mom thanking him in a high, tense voice. Finally, I went over to Roland and pulled his arm—which was reaching out toward the door in a way that looked uncomfortable—down to his side. He let it hang and said nothing.

"Roland, it's me. Can you hear me?" He showed no reaction, saying nothing, not moving. His eyes looked full of fear.

I turned to my mother. "Call an ambulance. Now." And she did.

We waited in the living room, my parents almost as stationary as Roland. Roland hadn't moved since I'd pulled his arm down, and if you couldn't tell he was breathing, you might have mistaken him for a mannequin. Finally, the intercom buzzed, and men in white coveralls with the insignia of Bellevue Hospital on the sleeve arrived. Roland made a small, strangled noise, and I leaned forward to hear it.

"Help. Me. Help," he said.

"We are here to help you, sir," one of the medical personnel said.

"Help. Me," Roland repeated. "Jesus help." He looked at Mom.

"Yes," my mother said. "Jesus sent me here to help you get into the hospital ambulance and take you where we can help."

Roland didn't move. One of the hospital men took his arm gently; Roland swayed but retained his strange posture. The medical guy nodded to his colleague, and the two opened a collapsible wheelchair and pushed Roland into it. My mother went with him. Later, she told me she'd sat with him in the emergency room for hours, and he'd murmured "help, help" in that strangulated whisper, asked her who she was and whether she was his girlfriend.

"I knew something was wrong," she said, looking into her coffee as we sat in the kitchen. "I'd asked him, the other day, what the clock said. When he answered," she paused, her voice shaking, "he said, 'The clock has no mouth.'"

A few days later—we were made to wait until he was stabilized—we went to visit Roland on the ward, Mom, Dad, and me. We had to go through two locked doors and were asked to open our bags and purses, and we were told that no sharp objects or medicines or drugs of any kind were allowed on the ward. The staff was friendly but extremely watchful. The lights on the ward glared as I entered; the linoleum floor was gray. The high windows had heavy wire gates, but there was sun. The smell, a curious, unpleasant mix of disinfectant with a powerful, plastic-like aroma and every bodily function imaginable, pervaded the ward. Wild-eyed, filthy homeless men, hair going in all directions, wandered the halls. A grandmotherly woman whose tired, sweet face seemed ordinary and pleasant smiled at me, but when she walked away, I saw her hospital johnny was completely open in back, revealing her excreta-encrusted naked backside. Other patients drooped apathetically in chairs by the window, some in lethargic poses that reminded me of my brother, a few with cigarettes posed in shaking hands, their knees jigging.

When we found Roland, he was lying on his bed in his room, looking less frightened and stiff. We knew that he had been tranquilized because we'd seen a nurse pushing a cart down a hall with plastic cups containing assortments of pills for each patient. While we were there, she handed Roland one of those cups and a glass of water and said in a friendly, no-nonsense way, "Now, Mr. Knox, time for your good medicine!" He took the pills, and she watched to make sure that he swallowed them.

"How are you?" I took his hand.

"Would you bring me a hat? A bowler hat?"

"You want a bowler hat," I said, so stunned by the sight of him and the hooting and shrieking outside his door that, momentarily, I could not remember what a bowler looked like.

"And when I get out, I might be a policeman," Roland said.

I felt cold, then numb, and as if I would never feel anything again. I had brought my dance bag with me—I had a class in half an hour. I said good-bye to Mom and Dad, who were going to stay a while, and I headed out. When I got past the second set of locked doors, I felt some trouble breathing and realized that I might cry. I swallowed hard and told myself that it was ridiculous, that he was in good hands—I could see that—and that he was safer in the hospital than he could be anywhere else. Outside of the hospital, where the sun was shining and some children were throwing snowballs, it occurred to me that he was locked up and I was free to go. I stood outside for a moment, telling myself to calm down. A nurse from his ward happened to come out at the same time and recognized me. My face must have shown my distress.

"Is this the first time you've visited your brother?"

I nodded and, to my horror, burst into tears.

"You've got to be strong! You've got to be strong!" she urged. She took my arm and pulled me down the steps. "Those people look strange, but they are all being treated, and they are all improving. I see them every day, and I know your brother is being helped."

"I know that," I said. "I'm sorry."

"It's a shock, I know," she said. Her sympathetic smile made it harder for me to control that tidal wave of sorrow that seemed to threaten to wash me down First Avenue. My throat hurt with the effort, and I turned and walked to Lexington Avenue and the subway, feeling astonished at how sad I was, and at how much I wanted to escape from feeling—from all feelings. As I strode down the grimy, dusty steps into the subway—it was a very cold day, and the wind swirled the grit around—I found myself beating down another fear: what if I became as crazy as my brother?

I told Dr. Sternbach about our Christmas, and he listened without interrupting, shrugged, and said, "They don't expect to cure him. You can't expect it either. He will not get better."

For a long time, I had known this, but I hadn't put it into words. There was no cure for my brother. I started to cry.

"Look—no cure does not mean no hope. I remember an old and famous professor from Vienna. He had seen patients in Europe and patients here in New York. And he told me a story. There were three patients. All schizophrenic, all incurable. Each one of them had been in the ward for twenty years. The hospital was experimenting with snake venom as a cure, and one patient was treated with snake venom. The patient fell into a coma, and they worried that he might die. Then he came out of the coma, and he was well enough to live outside the hospital. The second patient was accidentally hit on the head when a beam in the ceiling that was being repaired fell, and he also became unconscious. When he awoke, he was better. The third patient improved without any treatment."

"That's . . . hope?"

"There is no cure. Anything can happen."

I lay on the couch wondering what *would* happen to my brother.

"Roland never wanted for my parents to get divorced," I said. "*Ja, ja.*"

"I used to always think he was so calm. At the dinner table, he never got upset. I got upset, and he sat there like Buddha."

"Your brother is not calm. This is not the divorce or something you did or your mother did. This is what he was born with—he is like your father."

A chill went through me. "But could I be like him?"

"There is always a risk. These things run in families. I do not think you will become like your brother, but the genetic risks are high."

On the way home, I rummaged in the used book bin of the local bookstore until I found a few medical textbooks about schizophrenia. One said the disease would either appear by age twenty (but some books seemed to say thirty) or not at all. I thought I ought to search my mind for delusions, but wondered how I could even begin to ward off the condition. The very nature of craziness meant that I would be unlikely even to perceive symptoms. I would, I assumed, come down with odd thoughts like "people are reading my mind," and start imagining that these delusions were reasonable, and after that, I'd slowly lose every shred of sanity. I, too, could end up in a locked ward—or my children, if I ever dared to have them. But I didn't want them, I reminded myself: Dr. Sternbach had told me so, had told me now to focus on my education and my career.

FIFTEEN

Basement Missives

> The disclosure of the document to a third person,
> who shall be nameless, would bring in question
> the honour of a personage of most exalted station.
>
> E. A. POE, "The Purloined Letter"

The summer after college, I spent weeks at my Aunt Gwen's summer home. Ceci and I sat on the dock downing daiquiris, gazing at the slightly oily water—and as the hours slipped by, at the neon, air-polluted sunsets.

This is how I remember her: wry smile, bobbed hair laddered in elegant layers up the back, peach RELAX T-shirt draped over her swimsuit. Every day, we lay on the dock getting Coppertone all over *Vanity Fair* and the local papers, talking about old boyfriends, until she came up with ways to relieve the boredom.

"How about exploring the basement?" she asked one sunburned afternoon. "Discovery, here we come."

An old red canoe filled with water from winter flooding and mildewed sweaters in cartons seemed the sole revelations, until we came across a warped bureau whose drawers stuck. When we pried them open, we found family letters dating back to the 1930s.

"Get a load of this." My cousin handed me a faded blue envelope. Gaga was trying to talk my mother and aunt out of working in a tutoring center for "poor Negroes": "They have congenital syphilis, which you will get if they're climbing all over you, and THIS WILL INTERFERE WITH YOUR COLLEGE COURSES!"

"A blueprint for the letters our mothers send," I said.

"For their singular mystique." She smiled.

Aunt Gwen, age ten, writes from summer camp: "Please send me my party shoes, mommie, I really need them; and don't send candy, I'M NOT ALLOWED!"

"Gee," said my cousin, leafing through the letters.

"What?"

"See for yourself." She handed me another one from Gaga to Aunt Gwen: "I've never understood your temperament as well as your sister's. But there's no need to insult me!"

"Because your mother needed her party shoes?"

Ceci shrugged. "You knew Gaga only had my mum to keep yours company. My mum called your mother the little angel child."

"Gaga played favorites—?"

"Drink up." She handed me a beer.

Gaga had loved my mother more? Did that mean Gaga had loved me more than she'd loved my cousin? But Ceci never acted jealous.

I told her my secrets, things I shared only with Dr. Sternbach, who of course demanded I confide in no one but him.

Unlike him, my cousin was sympathetic; at least, she listened so hard that I had a hunch she might have gone through the same experiences. But when I look back, I see that she seemed more eager to hear my stories than to tell her own.

"Listen," I said. I told her how my father used to come into my room at night.

"Tell me!" She listened.

"So the same happened to you?"

"Oh, no!" She shook her head, laughed. "But Dad would get so drunk he'd tear off his clothes and run around yelling in the snow. One of us would have to get him indoors and back into clothes. Or—"

"Or what?"

She paused, as if thinking over her memories. "Get him on the toilet. Get him off the toilet. The next morning, he wouldn't remember anything."

"But you remembered."

She did not answer, offering me another beer. I didn't want beer—I wanted to talk. I wanted to ask about the time when she thought her Dad had been abducted by aliens. When I reminded her, she smiled and said she'd been eight years old so hadn't realized he was drunk. Waving another beer at me, her manner ever jovial, she winked and changed the subject. Grace went around saying "I hate Dad" to anyone who would listen. But Ceci just retired to her room and shut the door.

Another time, we went skinny-dipping. We drove to the beach at sunset, thinking we'd find it empty. Instead, we discovered a clambake version of Lover's Lane.

"We'll walk farther down!" she said, and we did, wincing from too-sharp pebbles and branches in our path as we hiked farther than we'd anticipated, sandals in hand. It got dark. We came to a wooded beach area, only to hear two lovers laughing. On we plodded, the feeling that we had to squeeze out an adventure driving us. By the time night had fallen, we'd come to an empty expanse—broad, moonlit, white-sanded, free of trees.

The only problem remained a wire fence extending into the waves. The fence could be climbed, and as we jumped from the top into the soft sand, I noticed a long, low, white edifice up the beach—an institution, maybe a hospital?

"Oh, we can't go here," she said. "That's the convent."

"Aren't the sisters sleeping?"

"Possible, possible."

"Let's teach those nuns how to *live*!"

Laughing, we threw off our sundresses and underwear and ran into the water, the moon rising. We swam to our hearts' content, then made our way back to the beach, our legs heavy as beached whales. I wondered if we'd manage an amble back to the car.

Just as we'd cleared the shore and stood yawning in the cool breeze, a siren howled and a massive searchlight flicked on. Floodlit, naked, blinded, we scrounged for our dresses, which we'd dumped in the dark seaweed. My dress was white, so I found it. Hers was black, blending right in with the seaweed. Our teeth chattering in the ear-splitting din, our eyes clamping shut, even as we forced them open in the stark light, we finally found her dress.

We ran. I have never climbed a fence so quickly nor sprinted so fast, jogging barefoot over those sharp stones, since we dared not take time to don our sandals. That siren kept blaring, even after we'd cleared the fence and made it to the car. Collapsing in my seat, I gasped, "Thank God."

She chuckled softly. "Don't get your knickers in a twist."

She took her time putting the car in gear, backed out as though we had all the time in the world. Smirking, she drove us to the beach house. I wondered at her amazing calm.

Though I didn't realize it at the time, my white dress and Ceci's black one signaled the inevitable collapse of our friendship. I wanted to see and be seen, and she wanted herself and all else hidden.

One evening, after Aunt Gwen had gone to bed, Ceci reminisced about her parents' divorce.

"She finally did tell Dad to move out." Ceci raised her glass in a toast and drained it.

"Wow!" I gulped mine down, too.

Ceci rolled her eyes. "He'd made all six of us sit around the dining room table, told each of us to look him in the eye and asked whether we wanted him to leave. We each looked him in the eye, said yes, Dad, *I want you to leave*."

"What happened?"

"He said, well, I'm *staying*!" She slapped her knee. "He'd never leave his meal ticket." Like my mother, my aunt held the purse strings. They poured cornucopias into the pockets of husbands whose contempt matched the size of the gift. Mom offered handouts to her adoring crowd, lonely young women culled from painting or dance classes, or who lived down the hall, all of whom found her charming. Unless you're a family member, she's delightful. Acolytes expressing gratitude for one gift got another. I always found it sad that Mom wanted to purchase worship. When I visited her, I found notes lying on tabletops—it seemed she wanted me to see them—addressing her as "Dear, dear, dear" and signed "Love, love, love." If only I admired her, everything would be OK.

Months later, Ceci and I united over Thanksgiving dinner when her sister Grace, who had announced she'd like an American Thanksgiving, fell back on the couch complaining. "Oh! Cooking that turkey! I just can't!" she sighed.

"Too stressful," soothed Mom.

"So much preparation," echoed Aunt Gwen.

"We'll order in a little Chinese food!" chirped Mom. "I can just have leftovers! I'm happy with my breakfast toast!" Her eyes went wide. "Would you like some espresso? I can make it! I'll just have instant myself."

I thought of previous Thanksgivings with Mom—one year, a wooden spoon left lying on a burner ignited, a merry blaze beginning before the smell of burning fat made me run into the kitchen, Mom annoyed, insisting I was ridiculous to worry. Then the time she forgot to turn the oven from preheat to bake. Another year, she wanted to use a twisted wire clothing hanger to prop up the turkey.

This year, Ceci and I got our massive bird in the oven, she gloating over "knobs of butter" with which she lavishly decorated it, while stirring swedes and carrots, thick with cream and pepper. She made potatoes and most of the vegetables. Neither of us wanted to slide into the family inertia: making that dinner, especially for her, whose brother was known as "Captain Entropy," meant forging a new family—a dynamic one that could triumph over our mothers and ensure that my cousin and I, if no one else, would rise from the ashes.

I made cranberry-orange sauce and corn muffins, plus a few pies. The board truly groaned, with all the muffins and sweet potatoes and Brussels sprouts and pies, the relatives and friends eating everything, because it all tasted so great.

My cousin and I smiled at each other across the table.

"My goodness, I don't see how you did all this!" squeaked Mom, affecting delight, her face a mask of horror.

"Have some!" I smiled.

"Oh, I couldn't possibly eat all that!" She pushed the food away. Later she ate off my plate, a slightly annoyed look in her eyes.

SIXTEEN

The Real Thing

> With such a tempest, as when Jove of old
> Fell down on Danaë in a rain of gold.
>
> THOMAS CAREW, "A Rapture"

Orgasm came, so to speak, late—when I was twenty-two, some eight years after Sternbach began instructing me to rub my clitoris and I began to picture him sitting beside the bed telling me I was doing it wrong. For the first time, I was living away from home, away from my mother, in an apartment with a lock on the front door to which she did not have the key, although she had asked for it. I was house-sitting for the summer.

Back in the city from Aunt Gwen's beach house, I had run into Jean, a neighbor of whom I was fond. Her own longing to escape, and her partial success, appealed to me. You'd never guess who she really was. Jean wore Birkenstocks, Guatemalan peasant wraps, and a most earnest expression. She and her husband, both academics, had a house filled with books. Huge rubber and leafy ficus trees lined the picture windows facing the Hudson. Furniture from the Salvation Army, including a battered fold-out on which I was to sleep, and a used TV, occupied the living room.

But the two of them were sitting on a railroad baron fortune and a rack of prestige, including an ancestor who'd been a famous American president. I didn't know it at the time, but they were listed in *Fortune* magazine among America's richest, their families prominent descendants of the Four Hundred. Jean and her husband were always afraid somebody would find out who they were and kidnap their kids. They had even founded a carefully integrated school on the Upper East Side that offered full scholarships to underprivileged nonwhite children. Jean's kids attended the school, and Jean and her husband paid for everybody. I had often babysat Jean's four children, who were now in their early teens. I'd occasionally watered plants for them when they were away for a long weekend. When Jean asked if I'd consider house-sitting for them, living in the apartment, sleeping on their Castro convertible in the living room, watering their plants, and just making sure everything was OK while they vacationed for two months at the family compound in Maine, I said, sure! I tried not to sound too eager, but the look of ecstasy on my face must have been prominent.

Jean gave me no instructions apart from plant watering, and I found myself and the loud echo of my footsteps in a gigantic Upper West Side apartment with a good ten empty rooms—the children's rooms, the master bedroom, the guest room, the playroom, the long hall, and all those bathrooms (seemed like there were two or three), and then the living room and a huge eat-in kitchen.

The kitchen rattled me. There was food in the fridge that I was sure would not last for the eight weeks they were away. Was I supposed to leave it alone? Eat it? Jean hadn't said. The freezer was filled with porterhouse steaks. Should I just leave them there? Would they rot or something? I phoned Jean, who sounded glad to hear from me. She was hoping I was comfortable in their home. I said I was—very. What should I do about that food and those steaks? Oh, eat the food, of course, said Jean. The steaks would be fine in the freezer, she said, very matter-of-fact. I hung up, feeling greedy and foolish, until I realized that she hadn't a clue that I'd been hinting. Even I hadn't realized I'd been hinting until I got off the phone. I was lusting after those steaks and hoping she'd guess that, but she'd really just been straightforwardly answering my question. I'm sure she would have invited me to eat them all if she'd understood that I wanted even one. Of course, there was no reason those things wouldn't keep for six weeks or six months. Maybe I'd been lonely, so lonely I was hoping she'd give me something. It was lonely. But I didn't have to say good morning to anyone, or hello. I didn't have to anticipate Mom's moods. I could indulge my own. I could just lie around. I was alone, and no one could see me. I took off my clothes and walked around the house looking at the family photographs on the walls. There were celebrities, mayors and presidents and national security advisors, labeled photographs of upright New Englanders with names like "Chauncey."

I'd seen that photo collection but never really looked at it on other occasions when I'd come down to babysit. Jean had waved at them once and said with considerable embarrassment, "We keep them on the walls for when the relatives come, and we try never to visit the relatives. Actually, we kind of have to go there nearly every summer to the big family compound, but you know that that's not who we are." She explained that her husband wanted the photos up for the relatives because he was sure they'd be offended if the photos weren't there. But neither of them wanted the kids exposed to the way of life pictured in those photos.

It was then that I'd realized how afraid she was I'd blow her cover. Not many people realized who they were and just how much money they had. You really couldn't see through their thick disguise until you saw all those photos on the walls of their apartment.

I had a feeling I understood what she and I had in common— we were perpetually running away from home. Her wonderful apartment was her hideout, a place to escape her burdensomely illustrious, fantastically wealthy family. Now I could think of her home as my castle, really my fortress, that would hide and protect me from my incredibly bizarre family. For eight whole weeks, it was to be mine, mine, all mine.

The first time I went down to their apartment, I took a suitcase with all the clothes I'd need, plus some laundry detergent. I could always go to my family's apartment and get things. But I hoped not to set foot once in the old family apartment. My mother had asked if I'd give her an extra key "for emergencies," and I'd told her that Jean and her husband had specified that their key should never be copied under any circumstances. The thought of Mom having a key filled me with dread; I found it hard to breathe when she asked. Mom looked disappointed— actually her face drooped with sadness—but she was well aware of who they were, too, as were a handful of people who lived in the building, so she did not question me.

Alone at last and loving it, I went to bed at eight for three nights and slept through until eight the next morning. After a few days, I felt like myself again and began to enjoy sitting in those high-ceilinged, bright rooms. I spent many mornings reading in the large, sunny living room. My afternoons and evenings were devoted to ballet and jazz dance. In the living room at night, I unfolded my bed and gazed at the dark Hudson and the flashing glimmers of light from the George Washington Bridge. I looked across to New Jersey, remembering Palisades Amusement Park, which I had visited as a child with my family. I got into the habit of walking around naked, although in the first few days of my glorious solitude, I would get scared and make sure the front door was locked. My mother was upstairs, some six stories above, I had to admit to myself, but it became easier to forget that as the days went on. I told Dr. Sternbach's group all about my new apartment.

"She can't see through walls," said Erik, the lawyer.

"Don't invite any strange men to visit," said Dr. Sternbach.

"I don't even know anyone I'd want to invite at this point," I said. The conversation had been fun up to that moment. I wanted someone to fall in love with me, and Sternbach always seemed to think that all I wanted was sex. I got into long discussions with him about sex being a part of love, but because neither were part of my life at that point, I usually took his word for it that I didn't know much about either.

The huge relief of my life at that point was that Mom didn't know when I was home, and I didn't know when she was home. I could almost forget about her. She did phone from time to time, and I let the phone ring when I thought she was calling. I lay on that sofa in the evenings watching TV. Sometimes I bought pints

of key lime pie ice cream from Baskin-Robbins and ate them while watching *I Love Lucy* reruns. I listened to the answering machine, called Jean whenever anyone left a message for them, and sat through incoming messages from my mother: "So how are you, dearie? I just was wondering what you're doing. Are you mostly dancing these days? And Melissa—I hope you got my messages. Do you know where the fire escape is in that part of the building? You know it's on the other side? Can you hear me? Are you aware of where that fire escape is at all? I do hope you know where it is in case there is a fire. And do you have a package of baking soda open by the kitchen stove in case of fires? And—" I turned the machine down so I didn't hear the rest of the message, and as soon as I heard the machine click to a stop, I pushed the delete key with a great feeling of peace.

I only heard from her when she wanted to ward off the dangers she imagined, and she tended to imagine them a great deal when things were going well with me. Once that idea came to me, I felt less guilty about not being in touch with her as much as she seemed to want.

One morning, I was lying on that fold-out bed, which was amazingly comfortable, loving the sight of the sun coming through the leaves of several large rubber trees. Broad, flat, beautiful leaves almost glowing with light. I sighed and stretched. I wasn't hungry. I didn't have to go anywhere. No one knew I was here or could find me. I felt warm—very warm. I lay on my back and gazed at the plants and the light and shadow on the ceiling. I let my hand rub the sheets and blankets, and then it found its way to my thighs. It was nice to stroke them . . . my hand worked between my legs. I closed my eyes and a scene played out—a tall, cruel man in black throwing a girl on her back. She'd been bad, very bad. He was tying her down . . . I touched my breasts. Something was building, building, I was breathing harder, rolling waves of pleasure growing more and more intense. A lovely sensation of something pulling from deep within flooded me, before there was a bursting of pain that was the deepest pleasure I had ever felt, my hips jerking up off the bed, my body snapping—I thought of a pinball machine all lit up—lovely, just lovely, and exhausting. I fell back and lay there panting. So that was it. Aftershocks. A few little aftershocks. I figured out how to make it last a little longer. If I just pressed one finger on the side there . . . oh, and inside at the same time—and another aftershock.

Dr. Sternbach's group met two nights later, by which time I felt like an expert. I had the urge to dress up and put on pearls and a black rayon dress that I thought looked like silk. I wore this outfit to standing room at the opera. When everyone was in his or her chair, they all looked at me curiously, and I burst out laughing. Marcia, the legal secretary, was jigging her knee. It had been a bad week at the office, she started.

"Oh, wait a minute. Clearly something's new. A new boyfriend?" asked the young lawyer. "You look like you got laid."

"Nope," I said. "Actually, well, in a way—" Now a faint embarrassment seeped through my exhilaration, but I told them anyway. "I had an orgasm. Finally, I mean. A real one."

"Oh," said Hannah, the magazine editor, with a knowing smile, and gestured to my black dress. "Look! The little girl died."

I sat waiting. Maybe I'd expected a prize from Sternbach, some imprimatur qualifying me for relationships or marriage. But he sat nodding through the rest of the session before smacking his lips, slapping the armrest on his La-Z-Boy, and ending it.

SEVENTEEN

School Days

Taught to the tune of the hick'ry stick . . .

WILL COBB AND GUS EDWARDS, "School Days"

I got into the full-time MA program at Columbia, and Dr. Stern-bach was proud of me. He said so. My mother had bought an apartment across the street from her own Upper West Side one-bedroom, and I moved in there with a roommate.

"Finally you are doing something worthwhile," Dr. Stern-bach said. "None of this dancing and ridiculous things. Your mother indulged you." He had insisted that I quit dance, and now, though I longed to go, and tried to make a class every month or so, I didn't talk about dance with him. He'd said I was delaying my progress, and I told myself he must be right.

Orange and brown leaves, a few red, were swirling through Riverside Park on a cool autumn day. I walked in a roundabout fashion toward my ultimate goal: coffee and croissants at the Hungarian Pastry Shop with Annie, whom I'd met in a class called Renaissance Metaphysical Poetry. When asked to gloss Andrew Marvell's "vegetable love," she had suggested that any well-rounded meal included a vegetable, earning the laughter of people who'd read *The Elizabethan World Picture* and knew that "vegetable love" meant the ability to grow fast, like the gigantic tubers sported by Woody Allen's character in *Sleeper*. But none

of them could write like Annie. She and I hated structural-
ism and loved novels together. A feminist professor, intending
to insult her, had spat, "You should write fiction!" Annie had
smiled back. "Oh, I do! My first short story was just accepted
for publication!"

Annie shared my love of debunking literary and cultural critics, whom we lumped together as the "Emperor's New Clothes."
The critics we were supposed to like, the ones whose theories,
properly threaded through academic papers, brought fame and
distinction, baffled us. It was the department gossip that grabbed
our interest. The other students sat on the floor in the halls, paper
coffee cups poised as they seriously discussed the meaning of
terms like "the Author." Their pale, serious faces showed no
awareness that the approving nod for which they longed from
admired professors couldn't compete with the pickled livers
and paltry sex lives endured by their idols. Our fellow students
flipped out phrases like "the text is a tissue [or fabric] of quotations" and bent their minds to finding meaning in *aporia,* or
"meaninglessness," a term introduced by the French critic Jacques
Derrida. A book was never a book but rather a text, and meaning
could never be straightforward: these lessons Annie and I had
absorbed with increasing disbelief.

We were, it occurred to me as I ambled toward Riverside
Church, where I'd gone to kindergarten, the only grad students
who laughed when we read French psychoanalyst Jacques Lacan:

> I think where I am not, therefore I am where I do not think.
> I am not whenever I am the plaything of my thought; I think
> of what I am where I do not think to think.

That was funny—even funnier when you read it out loud—and
how out of breath with hilarity we'd been doing just that, sitting
at one of those small tables in the Hungarian Pastry Shop, where
I'd be in about half an hour, to have tea and the delightfully
crunchy croissants that came with a little paper container of
the best marmalade I'd ever had, tangy and sweet.

I was looking forward to our meeting but taking the long way
around because I was early: I'd come from a session with Dr.
Sternbach, and Annie still had another twenty minutes at her job

answering phones in the English department. On her first day on the job, she'd taken a call from Edward Said, author of *Orientalism* and numerous tomes, and asked him to spell his name.

"*Sigh-yeed*! *Sigh-yeed*!" he'd yelled, as if pronouncing his own name extra loud would make her realize who and how important he was. How could anyone not have heard of him?

"Put me on to Steven Marcus!" he'd said.

"I'm sorry, Professor Sigh-yeed," Annie had replied, "but he's not in his office at the moment."

"You go get him and put him on the phone!" Said bellowed, loudly enough for Annie to hold the phone away from her ear.

Finally, he'd condescended to spell his name, but screamed at Annie when she informed him that Professor Marcus, to whom he wished to speak, was still not there.

"I'm coming over there right now!" Said yelled.

"Well, be my guest," said Annie, "but he's still not here."

I looked forward to more of Annie's English department tales. She'd enjoyed her anonymity and presumed idiocy, a side effect of the southern accent she was rapidly losing, both of which gave her an ear to conversations held by those who assumed someone like her would never listen, or be capable of understanding. Gleefully, she stored up tidbits she later shared with me: the hotshot translator of the French critic Derrida, a woman Columbia had wooed and won by offering an endowed professorship, had a crush on Professor Said, who ignored her. The graduate student assistant was married to a man who beat her. Professor Tayler was having an affair with a girl in his Shakespeare class, and when she declined to sleep with him—as another student, who worked as a cab driver and happened to pick up the pair one night, told Annie—Professor Tayler read out in class lines from Andrew Marvell's "To His Coy Mistress": "'The grave's a fine and private place,'" he intoned, looking at the girl, "'But none, I think, do there embrace.' Isn't that right, Ms. Finch-Davies?" He smirked at the girl, who lowered her head and blushed, tears beading in her eyes.

Riverside Church kindergarten came before Dr. Sternbach, I was thinking, as I headed toward its Chartres-like façade. I often divided my life into before and after, or bad and good, the time before I knew and the time when I discovered everything with Dr. Sternbach. I remembered riding my trike around on the roof. I had learned so much from Sternbach. Without him, I would not be the person I'd become. I would probably be a hippie or a drug addict, he'd pointed out to me. I would not be in graduate school without Sternbach's help. How would I ever write papers without him? I wanted so much to be able to write. I glanced to my left at the wall dividing the upper and lower parks. My father used to set me on that wall when I was three or four, walking along and holding my hand, shoving me off it and pretending to let me fall, while actually keeping a firm grip. I'd been leaning against that very wall on my first date with Walt, whose eyes and face and aroma still came to me occasionally. I thought briefly of ballet class—I hadn't been to class in so long and still missed it very much; I felt as though I'd lost a lover. I tried to think about something else.

I went over to the wall, looked down at the bare trees and a few gray squirrels darting up them. Put my hand down on the rough stone. Glanced at my watch. Time to go. I crossed Riverside Drive and walked back downtown on Morningside Drive and Broadway, crossing to Amsterdam Avenue and meeting up with Annie just as she was entering the pastry shop. She turned to me with a wicked grin that promised stories.

Leaning forward conspiratorially as we stood at the counter waiting to order our croissants, she said, "You will not believe who called to complain that their salary just doesn't show enough respect—and this person is being paid two hundred thousand."

"Name?" the woman behind the corner smiled as if she'd like to hear the rest of the story.

"Desdemona," I said. The servers called your name after you'd sat down, delivering the food on little trays, and I enjoyed offering the first Shakespearean character who popped into my head. I'd written a paper on the betrayed and murdered wife of Othello, who was, according to Dr. Sternbach, "a whore." But she did get strangled.

Annie and I sat down, and she whispered the name of the professor who wanted more money.

"Think of one of us getting a tenth of that amount for a fellowship," I said.

"I wouldn't have to answer phones," said Annie. "But you don't need it, do you?"

I didn't, truthfully. I had a secretarial job, too, but my mother was paying for Dr. Sternbach.

"How's your psychoanalysis going?" Annie asked. "How long have you been going, by the way?"

I stiffened, sure she would never understand, but I told her. Ten years. More.

Annie stared. She'd arrived in New York eight months earlier from a Bible Belt town in Florida, where nobody had ever heard of psychoanalysis.

Annie took a tiny bite of her croissant and stared at me with concern. I smeared all of my marmalade over one end of mine and ate rapidly.

"Won't you get better and stop seeing him?"

Her words burned. But this was one of those moments when I preferred to think of her as a hick. A dumbo from Florida who didn't know anything. I felt my nostrils flare.

"It's a process," I said. "It takes a long time."

"But—" Annie's eyes widened. "Isn't the goal to get to where you don't need a shrink?"

"You really don't understand," I said, sitting up rod straight. "It takes years even to get to the point where you start to understand your own defenses. Conscious life is just the tip of the iceberg."

Annie shook her head. I'd been hoping to impress her, but her look suggested complete disbelief.

"He's helped me get to the point where I can write papers." I knew I could not do that alone. Annie could write, something I envied tremendously.

"You know how to write on your own," I said, "but I have a lot of trouble."

Annie's eyes continued to express astonishment. "But Melissa, I've seen you in class. You're smart—you see things. You say intelligent things. You understand just as much as the rest of us. You knew more than I did about the Renaissance background." She stopped, considered, took another bite of her croissant. "I don't think you need this Dr. Stern, or whatever his name is, to help you with graduate school."

"You really have no idea what you're talking about," I said. I thought of Dr. Sternbach telling me I'd never be able to function without his support. I was psychotic. Nobody else could tell, but he was the only one who could help me. He'd said so.

"Well, I guess you know best," said Annie.

Within a few minutes, we were back to who was sleeping with whom among our meager collection of graduate student friends and professors. Who was getting which fellowship. Who would get to teach Freshman Comp or Lit Hum the next semester. Our argument was forgotten.

EIGHTEEN

Marriage Material

> All women become like their mothers.
> That is their tragedy.
>
> OSCAR WILDE, *The Importance of Being Earnest*

Marriage was a topic I brought up increasingly with Stern-bach as I emerged from my twenties and entered my thirties.

"You! You *always* pick the wrong guy!" he said.

"But why?"

"There is a psychotic core," he said. "You are not warm. Your mother! Your mother is warm, but you are not." He shook his head.

I left feeling an utter failure but very glad my cousin Ceci was moving to New York. We were looking forward to the day when my roommate moved out so Ceci could move in. Ceci and I had enjoyed a day of shopping in Chinatown, and I'd helped her move into her first apartment, a strangely dark, cramped room in the home of a large, asthmatic woman whose kitchen boasted a row of flour, sugar, and bean jars, each covered by a quilted tea cozy in the shape of a rooster. Ceci couldn't stand her wheezing landlady coughing around the kitchen and imposing rules about cooking, so I called a guy I knew from college who had a temporary sublet available, and Ceci went to meet him. He called me an hour later, desperate to see her. She'd probably responded with the noncommittal politesse I so envied; I couldn't talk to a man I considered remotely attractive without shivering and sweating.

So now he'd rented her the place, again in high hopes of dating her.

She told me she'd signed the lease. She added, with a grin, "I flirted with him to get the apartment."

I wanted to learn from her. Flirting was never a talent of mine; she knew how to do that, and she seemed to know how to do lots of other things I felt too incompetent to manage.

"Flirted with him how?" I'd never managed to flirt with the guy much myself, because I admired him, and that made me nervous.

Ceci shot me a curious look. "Well, it's easy. I just kind of smiled at him and winked a bit and said I might like to see him again." She shrugged. "That's it, really."

I nodded, knowing I'd never be able to do that. We went out that night to the local Chinese place. I'd just gotten my first credit card and didn't know how to use it.

"Don't you use a credit card, then?"

"Well, the terms and conditions letter makes it sound more complicated than taxes."

Ceci laughed. "Give it here." I handed her the automated letter, and she skimmed it. "It's really easy," she reassured, explaining that all I had to do was hand my card to the waiter and sign the little piece of paper and then pay at the end of the month.

Shortly before Ceci moved in to my apartment, I threw a dinner party. My friend Annie, away on a scholarship, asked me to include her fiancé, who would be lonely without her. I invited him.

Ceci brought him a glass of wine and before I got the meal on the table was already draped over him. A hooker with a heart of gold, she always seemed to understand without judging—but she could never be trusted around anyone else's man. It had yet to dawn on me that she never feared rejection because her heart wasn't involved in any of her flirtations. I thought her daring, bold.

I pulled her into the kitchen, said "hands-off-the-merchandise-he's-my-best-friend's-fiancé."

"OK!" She offered a salute, the private to the general. But she cocked an eyebrow, so I knew she felt annoyed. He was fair game as far as she was concerned—who was I to tell her what to do? She'd leave that to him.

When I came in with dinner, she had her head on the fiancé's shoulder and was plying him with wine. He sat stonily in his chair, but my cousin is awfully pretty. By the end of the meal, I heard, "Oh, please, take me uptown! I'm *sooo* bored! It's late—I need a ride home! Won't you take me?"

I could see the man's embarrassment, but also his attraction to her. He smiled. He felt flattered.

Annie would kill me. She would wonder whether I'd set up a meeting between Ceci and her fiancé on purpose. But I envied my cousin's freedom—I'd never have her guts.

I admired Ceci. Her enthusiasm at the sight of recherché boutiques, her bloodhound's nose for the perfect chocolate vol-au-vent, her lunatic, satiric humor that kept me in stitches—these remain with me even now, more than a quarter-century later.

When Ceci moved in, we shared stories every evening. The Wall Street traders she coped with, my alcoholic magazine editor boss, and adventures that only the two of us could have.

"So the receptionist at the front desk called this afternoon, sounding nervous," I began as I tossed a salad and she got the wine.

"Meanwhile, my boss advised his drinking partner he'd make their opponent roll over and get fucked," Ceci said.

"Oh, God. You're standing there?"

She shrugged. "They usually find me invisible. What's your story?"

"I wanted to be invisible this afternoon, believe me," I said. "My boss wasn't so happy with me—I'd made some typos and he'd had a three-martini lunch—and when the front desk called, I thought I was in trouble. And I was, but not the kind I thought." Then I imitated our receptionist: "Uh, there's, uh, a gentleman here to see you? You should, uh, come to reception?"

Did I hear a titter in the background?

"Not the receptionist's titter," said Ceci, who had already figured out who my gentleman caller was.

I wasn't dating anyone, but I'd been thinking, "It can't be. Don't let this be happening. It just can't. I'll lose my job." I walked the long hall toward reception. From twenty feet away, I could tell the person swaying with mirth in front of the desk—while the receptionist hunched over her noisy IBM Selectric as though she'd like to dive under it—was Mom.

In a newsboy's cap and a fake handlebar mustache, Mom swung her arms around, laughing. Uproariously.

"Pretend you don't know me!" she called in a loud, unconvincing Italian accent as I walked, then jogged, toward her. I smiled at her, wishing I could snap my fingers and make her vanish, along with everyone's memory of having seen her—including my own. Grabbing her elbow, I tugged her, unwillingly, out into the hall, where one or two secretaries on their way to the bathroom glanced at us blankly.

"She thought she was great—hilarious," I told Ceci, who nodded, knowing exactly what I meant. Nobody else did.

A pretty blonde, Ceci had on one of her first dates with her husband-to-be given him a naked-lady pen. It looked like an ordinary ballpoint but pictured—under see-through plastic casing—a shapely girl in a bikini who appeared to hail from the 1940s. Her lips remained fixed in a bright red pout. Hand on hip, one high-heeled foot poked provocatively in front of its mate, she posed like Betty Grable advertising cheesecake. When you tilted the pen, the bikini fell away, *and there stood a naked lady*!

My cousin, her boyfriend, and I had giggled over the pen. Dr. Sternbach, when I revealed this, became apoplectic.

"She is aggressive, this cousin of yours! This pen is like *stripping* in front of a man! *This* will not get you anything! This will not get you *love!*"

So forceful was he that I almost did not buy, for one of my boyfriends' birthdays, a pop-up version of the *Kama Sutra* that tickled me. Snorting with laughter, my cousin and I bounced the book open rhythmically, nearly breaking the spine, to see the inventive instructions—in all their three-dimensional glory—on inserting *lingams* into *yonis*.

The deal I'd made with myself was that I didn't care that much about the particular boyfriend, another graduate student younger than me, for whom I'd purchased this book. His youth and poverty rendered him ineligible, according to Sternbach, so I might as well enjoy my purchase—over which my cousin and I chortled ourselves silly before I gift-wrapped it, tied it with a big red bow, and gave it to the boyfriend, who was delighted. By the time I'd handed it to him, I'd already resigned myself to fifteen minutes of outraged criticism from Sternbach, whose face was so red I thought he'd have a heart attack.

But that was nothing compared to the general topic of marriage.

"Marriage is a terrific task for young people!" he would begin, the fist slamming the end of the couch. The most psychologically healthy person in the world would find unexpected challenges.

Therefore shall a man leave his father and his mother, and shall cleave unto his wife: and they shall be one flesh.

I did not want to leave Sternbach so that I could cleave unto someone else. Did I ever admit this to myself? Not at the time. Not for years. Not until I met the man who would become my husband. Not even then.

Sternbach shook his head. How little I knew! How lonely marriage was! So I thought I would have companionship? Laughter.

"I was *so* lonely during my first marriage," he reminisced, meaning the one that happened because he had to leave Vienna when Hitler came, the girlfriend he loved having dumped him. "And did I tell you about the time I got away from the Nazis by sailing to the Caribbean? And I brought my skis?"

I felt more and more at fault for not having experienced anti-Semitism firsthand, but I wanted very much to have a husband I loved, and I wanted to have children with him.

Since all non-Jews must be anti-Semitic, I felt I had to marry, or at least to date, a Jew. If I could marry one, I could somehow become a Jew, and then I would be considered cured.

"Just finish your PhD!" Sternbach would yell when I'd raise the issue of marriage.

"I will make a scholar out of you!" Sternbach had boomed sometime around the time I finished college. "You should be proud! You finished college! A girl like *you*."

I was glad I had pleased him, and I'd enjoyed my English classes. I had agreed to apply for graduate school while continuing to work for the magazine group that ultimately funded part of my master's degree.

"Oscar Wilde had wit! Oscar Wilde was a psychologist! You should read Oscar Wilde."

I hadn't read any Oscar Wilde—I'd mostly been reading seventeenth-century English religious poets, whom I immensely enjoyed. Dr. Sternbach did not enjoy them.

"You should write about Oscar Wilde!" Dr. Sternbach said one day.

I began working in a halfhearted way on a dissertation psychoanalyzing Oscar Wilde, Oscar Sternbach having chosen the topic.

In the group, he remarked, "Marriage would be great, if it weren't for the sex!" The group nodded. The married members bemoaned the lack of sex. The unmarried members bemoaned the lack of sex, too.

"We don't ask for perfect," Sternbach would nod sadly, when I insisted on discussing my desire for a husband. Repeating that I was "a very difficult girl," he intimated I would meet someone who could put up with me eventually.

"That would have to be a guy who could stand a demanding, anxious woman," said Martin, another psychoanalyst in our group. He was himself so depressed that—after electroshock therapy robbed him of his short-term memory, though not his depression—he began downing teacups of vodka before seeing patients. I thought his remark unfair, since I had taken my turn picking him up from his electroshock sessions, as had other group members, his estranged wife being in no mood to do so.

Sternbach concurred. Offering a tale of a marriage between two colleagues that had gone sour, he added, "They should have come to me! I could have helped them!"

I dated a Jewish guy for a while, and Dr. Sternbach said, "He's a poor Jewish guy from Newark!"

He made Philip Roth's hometown sound like the tenth circle of the Inferno.

That guy and I eventually broke up.

"Well, Melissa," said Erik, the lawyer, "if you've learned one thing from this group, it's better to be depressed because you aren't married than depressed because you are."

Unlike my analyst, my cousin sympathized when I spoke of my longing for a man who enjoyed holding hands. One of my boyfriends had always dropped mine with apparent distaste even when he seemed to want to kiss me.

"I want him to love me," I sobbed after a breakup.

She shrugged. When her eyebrows rose, I knew she thought me a fool for love.

"You can't really tell them stuff like that." She shook her head. "They figure you want a house and a disposable income."

"Is that what you want?"

She laughed. I longed for her total self-control, her take-charge attitude, and her ability to form a five-year plan. I always felt helpless around my feelings, which burst out all over the place. Indulgent when she saw me crying, she seemed above and beyond such storms herself. If only I could develop more maturity, more patience, I'd be serene, like her.

One day she came home from a date, knocked on my door, beckoned me with the canny look that I loved.

"I made him say it!" she said.

"What?"

"I made him say he loves me!" She waved her hand, flashing that glint of gold around her ring finger.

"So you're—going to get . . . ?"

"I told him I was just going out for a pack of cigarettes—that was our joke, but I acted like I meant it." Her eyes danced.

What was the matter with me? My heart was always too plainly dangling from my sleeve, and my cousin was going to live happily ever after. I was a bridesmaid, my feelings calamitous, because when I told my boyfriend I'd been dreaming about my cousin getting married, he bolted. My cousin and I shared everything, but now she would settle down to the American Dream in the suburbs, and I would dry up in Manhattan.

At her wedding, she was so nervous she felt physically ill, but she said that was normal, and I believed her. She got pregnant almost immediately and within two years became a nursing mom, an entire train ride away.

NINETEEN

At First Sight

Never did run smooth.

WILLIAM SHAKESPEARE, *A Midsummer Night's Dream*

The lobby of the Chicago Hilton on Michigan Avenue clanged with the sound of huge brass dollies trundling luggage into elevators, phones and bells ringing, loud talking, and my own thoughts crunching: I had traveled across a time zone and a number of mental blocks for a single job interview in a place far from New York. In the back of my mind remained the fear that any job would likely take me away from Dr. Sternbach, who shook his head. A friend who'd snagged an anything but lucrative job at a small southern college said, "They're paying me in Louisiana dollars," and my experience so far, a hateful year as a secretary, along with writing about half of a dissertation, qualified me for nothing but teaching.

The annual Modern Language Association meeting was about to take place, and students like me got a discounted rate for Hilton rooms—though not, I was to find, for Hilton breakfasts: two bagels with butter and jam and two coffees were to run my friend Annie and me close to thirty dollars. I wasn't relishing the thought of encountering hundreds of other graduate students desperately seeking jobs, most far more qualified than I felt—nor of attending talks with titles like "Jane Austen and

153

the Masturbating Girl." Where was Annie anyway, the friend with whom I'd braved most of my MA year?

Annie and I were sharing a room and had agreed to meet at check-in. My feet were freezing, it was snowing outside, and I had to pee. When I finally got to the window, I was told, "Oh, your friend checked in an hour ago." I lugged my suitcase to the elevators. As I was hauling out my key card, Annie opened the door.

"Hi," I said.

"I've met the perfect guy for you!" Annie's eyes held a gleam I knew all too well. Several other dates with perfect guys had been arranged for me by her and her husband. He had taken a photo of me and the man they'd hoped I'd enjoy meeting at the last one. The man and I were facing opposite directions—even our legs were crossed in opposite directions. We looked like a print ad for marriage counseling.

"Well, let's get something to eat first," I said, not at all eager to do anything other than collapse.

Annie looked me over calculatingly. "I know you. You can't think 'til you've eaten. I'll tell you all about it over dinner," she promised. As we sipped our red wine and twirled forks in our spaghetti, she relayed details of her layover in St. Louis, where she'd encountered an MLA-bound graduate student whom she was sure I would like. She gazed at me with that look of utter conviction I knew all too well.

"So he's very handsome," Annie offered, taking a bite of her roll. I nodded. She and I had never agreed on what constituted very handsome, and for the umpteenth time, I wondered how friends with such similar tastes in literature could differ so greatly in a department far more important.

"Big blue eyes!" Annie added. "Curly brown hair."

I took another sip of my wine, pictured a Ken doll, and smiled.

"At the airport while we were waiting," Annie continued, "he started flirting with me. He's clearly looking for a girlfriend. His accent's really cool—European and unplaceable, although I think he's from Germany. He invited me to spend the day with him at the Art Institute."

I nodded.

"So I said, 'I'm married, but you should meet my friend Melissa!'"

"You didn't!"

"Of course—why not? So we're meeting him tomorrow at the foot of the escalators. It's cool—it's not a date," she said hurriedly, seeing my expression. "He's bringing friends who are here for job interviews, too."

"OK!" I said. A day wandering around an art museum with a bunch of smart grad students sounded like a good way to gear up for the job interview I dreaded, and the talks I dreaded even more. I knew I should be writing talks like that, but I couldn't.

The dissertation I was writing with Dr. Sternbach was "psycho-analytic" in the sense that he thought my subject, Oscar Wilde, was very aware of the unconscious mind. I didn't use any of the contemporary psychoanalytic theorists, like Jacques Lacan or Julia Kristeva. Certainly not Otto Kernberg, even though my dissertation director had assigned him in class. I would bring these writers to my sessions with Dr. Sternbach, and he would tell me what he thought of them.

"Crazy! Absolutely psychotic!" he fumed after reading a paragraph of Lacan. I had to agree with him there—Lacan's jargon made no sense to me, and Freud was at least straightforward. Therefore my dissertation remained Freudian, although sometimes I pretended otherwise just to get along with people. "Oh, I'm interested in object-relations theory," I would say, hoping they wouldn't ask too many questions. I need not have worried. They were too busy worrying about their own dissertation directors, their own therapists, their pile of freshman English compositions to correct, if not the source of their next meal.

Four or five days a week, I went in to my session and read aloud from whatever chapter I was writing, or handed the pages to Dr. Sternbach. He sat frowning as he read, making pencil marks in the margins, and often demanded that I rewrite the whole thing. I believed that I was unable to write without his assistance, so I often left my sessions in tears.

I sighed and drank another glass of wine. It was good to be at the convention after all—maybe I would learn something, distract myself, or at least have a good time. Annie smiled.

The next morning, bundled in our warmest coats against the freezing, windy Chicago weather, we stood at the top of the escalator looking down, trying to spot Josef and his friends before descending. I was tired that morning, and almost ready to cancel with the excuse of a headache: I wanted to read a few student papers I'd brought along and dip into a David Lodge novel. I wasn't really in the mood to go traipsing around in such cold weather after all.

"Hey, Annie!" said a deep, pleasant voice, and I looked up. A hand waved from the bottom of the escalator; I saw a smile, a black leather jacket, a rakishly tilted beret.

Annie motioned for Josef to stay put at the bottom of the escalator as we started down. But he bounded onto the up escalator. As he neared us, I stared. He really did have bright blue eyes, rosy cheeks, a warm expression, and curly brown hair. He was the handsomest man I'd ever seen in my life, an impression confirmed when he glanced smilingly right into my eyes and I felt the kind of turbo-charged erotic impulse that I knew to tamp down on first dates. He waved at us, and when he greeted Annie cheerfully and said he'd be right back down, I felt a twinge of jealousy.

We met at the foot of the escalators, and Josef introduced some of the grad students he'd flown with from LA—they all looked even colder than I felt. We walked around the Art Institute, and I found myself gazing at him frequently. His calm, booming voice soothed people, as did his smile. He was a natural leader. People liked his suggestions. When we were done with the Art Institute, he mentioned a German restaurant in the area, suggesting we all go there.

"I can order for us," he said. "There's a special kind of beer—"

No one had to be asked twice. We followed him, and he led us to Berghoff's, where the waiter fell over himself accommodating us after Josef spoke to him in what, he explained, was a very polite Bavarian dialect. The waiter rushed in with tall glasses of Weizen beer, lemon slices floating on top, and some tender wiener schnitzel, also accompanied by lemon. On the side was something none of us had ever seen before that looked like some kind of fried dumpling or noodle. Spätzle, they were called, he said. The buttery crispness went perfectly with the meat. I wasn't used to beer in the middle of the day and began to chatter, telling every joke I could think of. Josef regarded me curiously, affectionately. As if he wanted to protect me.

"Of course these are really Viennese," he said, gesturing to the meat. "But Bavarians eat very similar dishes. Austria is very close to us, you know."

I did.

"I know someone Viennese in New York," I started to say and noticed his face go still. "An old man," I added. "He's very old."

TWENTY

A Whale of a Gift

Love me do

THE BEATLES

"Low Tide Whale" said the embossed cream card leaning on the blue-and-white pitcher. That inquiring expression in the whale's eye—it tempted me. He gazed upward at the spume blowing from his head as though questioning his thoughts.

I turned the pitcher over. "M.A. Hadley Designs" was fired into the bottom in swirls of blue. A price sticker indicated a sum beyond what I usually spent on birthday gifts. But my cousin Ceci, in a wistful moment, had wondered what had happened to her family's whale pitcher.

I thought of her with her new baby in her new house in the suburbs. We saw each other infrequently, but my single-spaced letter brimming with revelations about our mothers must be even now sitting in her mailbox.

I missed her laugh. I poured myself an imaginary orange juice.

As I gripped the handle of the pitcher, I could hardly wait for her to call and compare notes. I could see her smiling at my descriptions, eyebrows raised with delight at the way I'd put together the puzzle we'd been working on together for so long.

"I'll take it!" I said, handing the pitcher to the saleslady before I could change my mind, adding, to go with it, some whale stoneware cups.

Our lives had naturally separated after Ceci had gotten married. Having finished graduate school, I'd gotten an assistant professor job and then a fellowship to study biography. I often brought short stories or ideas about articles I wanted to write to Sternbach; he read them impatiently, urging me to sound more "bubbly" or sighing and saying they sounded flat. I returned to some of our family papers, both the ones my cousin and I had found in the basement together so long ago and others I'd found in libraries. Granddad had written letters to Anaïs Nin, whom he'd first met when she'd applied as a young woman to be an artist's model, and whom he'd painted and sculpted. She'd befriended my grandparents. When his own marriage was failing, when Gaga collapsed into tears daily, Granddad came to believe that Anaïs was the only one who could help her. His own analyst, Otto Rank, was having an affair with her, Mom told me, but he seems not to have known. His work appeared in galleries, was sold to Nin's followers, and eventually enhanced biographies of her. Nin became a family friend, invited to dinners and outings with her East Coast husband, Hugh. The letters to my grandfather sounded flirty, but my mother claimed he hadn't married or even had any sexual experience until he was forty, when he'd married Gaga, who was then seventeen. Was he closeted? Mom had once come to me giggling with a portrait he'd painted, asking, "Guess who?" The girlish face seemed vaguely familiar—a long jaw, soft, submissive eyes, a pompadour of brown hair heaped like Lady Astor's in the Sargent painting. When I couldn't identify the person, Mom revealed that it was Granddad, who'd painted himself as a woman.

When I'd told Ceci about Granddad in drag, she'd chuckled. But I'd waited to tell her all that I'd discovered, all that I'd planned. I wanted to write a book about the letters between my grandfather and Anaïs Nin. The idea percolated, and I plunged into research, visiting libraries, photocopying letters, and interviewing Nin's West Coast husband—who poured me a stiff margarita with which I poisoned a potted plant before enduring a wild car ride through Silver Lake to a restaurant where, despite pitchers of margaritas, I failed to learn anything more about Nin.

I tried a different tack. From a hotel room in Los Angeles, where I sat on a white chenille bedspread, photocopies of Nin's letters from the UCLA library and sheets of questions spread around me, I phoned Mom in New York, my mind filled with the earthquakes I feared. And there was one coming, but not in Los Angeles.

Mom's voice got spooky—as if she were in a trance. "Oh, no, Da wasn't gay."

"Why do you think that?" I asked.

"Oh. Well . . . he loved little girls. He painted Nin because she seemed like a little girl. He used to love it when little girls sat on his lap. He told them stories; he loved to see their eyes get all round. He and I were . . . chummy."

Her voice got even quieter. Although I was dying to ask exactly what she meant, some instinct made me keep silent. And then Mom continued.

"Well, if you want to get Freudian about it, there is something else I've never even told my sister. I was close to Daddy, and when I was little, I used to come and stand next to him and he would put his hand under my skirt and stroke my legs and bottom, but not on the genitals. I never thought there was anything sexual about it"—my mother's voice rose as she said this—"or had the feeling that he was aroused. It was just a close, warm feeling. And then when I was thirteen and I got my period, I realized that this would be awkward, and I withdrew, and he didn't try to do it again."

I marveled over my mother's confession—she'd actually remarked "I didn't want his hand to get all bloody," as if I needed that explanation to understand why her father's hand did not belong between her legs. As far as I was concerned, there was blood on his hands from way back and forever.

Ceci would go nuts for this. Everything about the sisters was coming into focus. Mom became the child who never grew. She dressed in baggy clothes that concealed her breasts, or she wore a newsboy's cap. Whenever I was sick as a child, she'd sit by my bed with an air of resentment, as if distressed by my failure to comfort her.

Cross-legged on that bedspread, speed-writing my questions and Mom's answers, I could not wait to talk to Ceci—the key we'd so long sought together had unexpectedly appeared and even turned in the lock. How had we failed to catch something so obvious that I could not believe we'd never thought of it? We'd imagined our fathers as completely different from Granddad. Our fathers drank, after all, and because Granddad teetotaled, we thought he must be different. We wanted him to be different. My memories of him remained dim: a soft-spoken, rueful face, a kind old man in a bow tie who'd died when I was seven and when my cousin was four. I remembered being angry with him for dying before I could give him a creature I'd molded from clay in art class and painted just for him. And here I was now, unveiling his great big clay feet.

My grandfather's portrait of himself as a priggish looking woman—no wonder. It was he who wanted to be *Very Much a Lady,* the title of his unpublished novel and the phrase he had used to describe Anaïs Nin when she first came to pose for him in 1922. A lady could remain as detached from sex as a nun. On a 1935 visit, Nin regaled him with her written accounts of erotic escapades with Henry Miller and others; Granddad wrote, "This affected my tummy and I thought I might 'fwow up.'" He was fifty-nine when he wrote this—and expresses himself like a five-year-old boy confronted with adults having sex. A child at heart, he seems to have found sexual satisfaction only with other children, alas, his daughters. Mom recalled his telling her, "Whenever your mother and I have *picnic,* she won't look at me over breakfast." Nothing went by its real name—"whenever ladies have sawdust," began my grandfather, attempting to explain to my mother why Gaga cried so much.

Our mothers acted like little girls because they felt like little girls. They'd never grown beyond the time when their father fondled them. I could understand that—in so many ways, neither had I.

As I ended my letter to Ceci, I speculated on what Granddad might have done to my aunt: Mom had so emphatically insisted

that Granddad could not possibly have touched her sister that I knew he must have molested my aunt as well. I urged my cousin to play the detective.

And what about that painting Granddad did of himself as a woman? Does your mother have anything like that? (And could you maybe collect this or any other piece of evidence before you ask her any question that might induce her to destroy it?) Even in my feverish enthusiasm, I got that our mothers had been keeping a very big secret for a very long time. What I didn't get was how much Ceci would want to keep the secret, despite or because it was such an open one—collectors of my grandfather's paintings and sculptures considered his pedophilia old news.

The day before I bought the whale pitcher, I'd sent Ceci the real present, the answer to our questions, that long letter revealing everything I'd learned about Granddad. I'd sent a book proposal too, outlining my thoughts on Nin's and my grandfather's letters. That ladylike manner of Granddad's, the aesthetic, unathletic tilting of the hand that I'd taken for gay in both my grandfather and father—with my own father, I knew better. Dad had a girlish manner. He'd come into my room, drunk, moaning, burying his face in my hair, weeping and stroking me from neck to ankles, lingering on my buttocks.

"Remember?" I wrote, picturing my cousin's raised eyebrow and delighted smirk as she read my letter. "Here's the bomb-shell!" I added.

This was my whale of a gift. Granddad was like our fathers.

For days after I'd mailed the package, Ceci neither called nor wrote. I didn't know what to think. I'd so hoped to please her with the whale pitcher and had looked forward to hearing her say she was happy to get one just like the one they'd had when she was seven.

I started to wonder whether she ever received the package, whether she might not have liked it, then whether she might be ill. Had something happened?

Finally, I called. "Hi, it's me."

I was waiting for Ceci's bright "hi!" Instead, I heard nothing—or someone catching her breath.

"You just got carried away, didn't you?"

"What?"

"I opened the envelope—the baby cried and I had to lay your . . . *letter* on the kitchen counter. What if the maid had read that thing?"

I was stunned. Her maid? Her illiterate maid? Her maid who didn't speak English?

"But—you remember what we talked about on the dock, right? Our fathers. The—the—just everything—makes sense now. Two molested sisters marrying—"

She cut me off. "It's a stretch." Her voice suggested the patience of a kindergarten teacher addressing a devilish child. Calm, with a faint hint of irritation. As if I'd told a tasteless joke, or a pointless one.

"But—"

"You wanted scandal. Or money. Curious, your wanting to write about Granddad." She took a breath. "Curious, not writing about your own father." A low, enraged tone had crept into her voice. I felt my heart race. I couldn't breathe. Was it really possible I had misunderstood?

"I thought you'd want to know! It's what we talked about on the dock, so often!" No, I hadn't misunderstood. I knew Ceci. Something had changed.

"This is family!" she said in a low voice. "I object!"

I so couldn't believe what she was saying that I felt like laughing, although I wasn't happy. A nervous giggle seemed about to erupt: I almost chuckled and stopped myself. Why would she now object to the truth, to a past we shared, to a mystery we both wanted solved? Unless. The question of how the past might be repeating itself began to form.

"You were asking me to spy on my mother!" Now she was yelling.

"But don't you remember all the things we talked about on the dock—?"

All the favorite moments of my life with her and with her siblings—these were the only times when I felt I'd found family: we had the same laugh, the same voices, the same gestures. We resembled one another. I thought of my cousins as previously undiscovered brothers and sisters, my own brother having long escaped into a world requiring antipsychotic medication and hospitals.

"I object! None of this is true about Granddad!"

She didn't remember how much we had talked. Or she did. I'll never know.

A day later, Mom called.

"Hi!" I said. "How are you?"

"You'll be hearing from me," she said, in a voice quivering with rage or sadness—it was hard to tell. Her voice was shaking, and she hung up. I held the receiver wondering if she'd actually meant to hang up, then replaced it wondering whether I should call, or she would call. She did not, I did not, and a feeling of tremendous foreboding increased all that day. Ceci would surely not have? I didn't even want to spell out the thought. But it was true: Ceci had mailed my letter to Mom.

Mom FedExed me that day: "I cannot blame you for lacking some instinctive perception of other people's emotions or moods, any more than I could blame someone for being colorblind," she wrote. "Possibly 'coping strategies' could be developed for fewer surprises, and smoother relationships." She was in Nantucket, and made a point of telling me I was not to enter her apartment while she was away. She wanted to see me with Dr. Sternbach when she got back. I was to apologize to poor Ceci. The memory, Mom wrote, of her own father "seemed so slight," but she had told it to me in order to help me with my research.

She had meant her confession as a *gift* to me from her. And I had betrayed her. I was "gossipy." I was "frivolous." I was "extremely irresponsible."

Scene: Dr. Sternbach's office. Couch. Upholstered side chairs, in which Mom and I sit. She leans forward so that she is almost in his lap, and she looks as if she is about to burst into tears. I sit with my hands folded in my lap. My stomach is so unsettled that I am afraid of vomiting. Dr. Sternbach stares at me with apparent disgust.

Mom, turning to me: "I feel that I really don't know you! I've never known you!"

Me: unable to speak.

Mom, turning to Sternbach: "You know, her father was always violent! When she was little, he'd say he'd tear the dress off her back!"

I let out a sigh and sit back. She wants a reason for not knowing me, an excuse, any excuse, and a good one. She wants to believe that because Dad had had tantrums, hit me, hit her, I had become a monster with no feelings who sent out letters about her and disturbed the whole family with my narcissism.

Sternbach, after Mom has left: "Your mother will forgive you."

Back in the Upper West Side apartment, every evening after work when I lived with my cousin, one of us would pop our Rosie Vela cassette into the tape player:

Livin' is only a Fool's Paradise.
I'm into somethin' and nothin' feels right.
Givin' is only to get somethin' nice . . .

Try as I might, I couldn't get my cousin to see what I saw—or at least not to admit it. I'd believed I'd had an ally, a sister. For all those years, I'd been the one who couldn't see clearly—yes, about Granddad, but also about my cousin. Nothing could be worse than discovering that the person on whose understanding I had pinned every last hope had never existed. I'd invented her, casting her in the role of big sister because I'd imagined she was calmer: I'd thought of her as a mom because I'd needed one.

Years later, it occurred to me that I resemble my cousin's mother far more than my own—she must have felt as though I were betraying her, talking about what her mother kept well hidden.

"Mum said he never touched her!" Ceci raged when I called to apologize.

"I see," I said.

"Putting your hand on a kid's bum is not sexual. Don't be ridiculous."

Not wanting to admit to myself at the time that I'd already lost my cousins—that really, I had never had the relationship I'd imagined—I apologized. For me, the younger generation of our family had always felt like an army building a better way of life than our mothers had experienced or provided: my cousins and I would collaborate in understanding the past to improve the future. Nothing could have been further from the reality.

"Let's put it behind us," my cousin said with an air of satisfaction. She had everything she wanted—the perfect house, the shiny kitchen, the husband who brought home the bacon. We both knew what was in those dusty boxes, and now we knew why, but the dream of discovery remained mine alone. I wanted the boxes wide open, the whole mess of the basement out on the dock, my mother's confession unfolded in the sun. My cousin wanted the secrets packed away, the dust undisturbed, the boxes deep in shadows. She wanted me out of her life.

I spent an afternoon in front of an open window, willing myself to lean out too far and let gravity take its course. Occasionally I pulled back in, called friends, reached only answering machines. I forced myself to shut the window.

I still long for that paradise in which, like identical twins, my cousin and I drank the same drinks, cocked the same eyebrow, cracked the same jokes. We stood shoulder to shoulder, warding off our mothers, giving each other strength. We had seemed a team, shaking our fists at stupidity, parsing our past together. If there's anything at all to the idea of redemption, my cousin had been that for me.

We would never again be a team. I would always miss her.

Aunt Gwen invited me to lunch and, wagging a finger, told me that she wanted to set me straight. Granddad had no sister. He'd painted himself as a woman because he wanted to know how his sister might have looked. That painting didn't have anything to do with wanting to be a woman.

Then came the reason for my lunch invitation: Granddad had never molested her, so he could not possibly have molested my mother, *right*?

I said I could not predict that, and my aunt started begging.

"Look, I told my children how wonderful my father was, because their own father was so terrible. You just can't take that away from people, hmmf? If you take that away . . ." Her voice faded. She was pleading with me. I saw in her expression that she was letting me know that I was right in all my discoveries. She, too, as a child had experienced a "special" relationship with her father, but she thought it was wrong of me to discuss it. "You know, Granddad is not your personal property," she snapped.

I'd brought with me a brown mailing envelope containing photos I never intended to show my aunt. I needed them as one needs in desperate situations some talisman—a crucifix, a mezuzah, a lucky rabbit-foot: those photos were my moral support. My grandfather had taken eight-by-ten black-and-white photos sometime in the late 1930s, and they showed my aunt and my mother naked on a beach in fluid, balletic poses like romantic woodland sprites; both girls were teenagers at the time, and their breasts and pubic hair showed. Imagine Maxfield Parrish teaming up with Lewis Carroll.

As my aunt's voice droned on, I became so afraid I'd believe her—and I partly wished that I honestly could—that I kept reaching over to my bag to pat the envelope with the photos.

Those were real. I could touch them and look at them. Yes, even if my mother, my aunt, my cousins, and the rest of the world told me I was wrong, I could look at those photos and reassure myself that I was right.

But pulling out those photos meant facing the inevitable loss: the complete break with my family.

Before the debacle, I'd asked my mother about the photos. With ferocious merriment, she'd said, "Oh, he wanted to take pictures of his daughters growing up." At that, I'd put them in an envelope, and I'd put the envelope in a safe place.

I'd *thought* they were in a safe place—but years later, I went through every file in my office and couldn't find them. Then I phoned my mother to ask if I'd imagined the photos or if they'd really existed.

"Oh, yes," she'd squeaked happily. "Mother wanted photos of us in the altogether, since we were growing up." Her father had indeed taken those pictures: "I was dancing with seaweed in my hands in the water!" She'd seemed proud.

But would she send them to me?

"Yes, when I find them." Then, "They might be a little X-rated for your children," she'd said, her voice thin and high.

When I found the photo of my mother dancing, it was just as I had recollected. What I had never observed is that my mother's eyes are closed. The sun was in them, yes, but what girl wants to see her father taking a photo of her naked fifteen-year-old self? How could she live with knowing she was displaying her breasts and pubic hair to him? According to Mom's note on the cardboard cover, her mother had wanted these photos taken.

I had one last visit with Mom in April 2017, bringing my now much older children, whom I'd briefed about her behavior. To my fifteen-year-old son, she'd remarked, "Oh? Are you fifteen? I remember when I was that age. I just wanted to sleep all the time."

She had slept through the years of awakening, and no wonder.

In the way that you press a bruise to see if it still feels sore, I still listen to that Rosie Vela tape my cousin and I used to play. I reminisce—the great escape from the nuns and their searchlight, the time we'd almost had to run home naked, hadn't thrown light on my cousin.

I had been the one to suggest that the two of us teach those nuns how to live—I wanted our mothers to know how to live. The way we, Ceci and I, knew how to live. Didn't we?

What could have been more absurd: at the very moment when my cousin had wanted me to play the mother and reassure her that Granddad had been nothing like our fathers, I had wanted her to play the mother, too, and pat me on the head for my wonderful discoveries. Meanwhile, our actual mothers continued to be permanently out to lunch—yet here we were, the seekers, the detectives, or so I'd thought, following in their footsteps, pushing into shadows the clues we'd thought we wanted.

Occasionally I still imagine my cousin pouring herself a glass of orange juice from that blue-and-white whale pitcher. I hope that the pitcher is still sitting on a kitchen shelf, still being used, not covered with dust. I'm glad I didn't pour myself out that window—instead, I have poured out these recollections, getting dusty in the process. Flipping through old journals, old letters, old photos, I found Anaïs Nin and a grandfather handsomer and younger than the one in my childhood memories. Beside him stand two little girls, my dark-haired smiling mother and my freckled, bemused aunt, Nin smiling down on her, as though realizing that her mother did not.

TWENTY-ONE

Burning Up

> I am bound
> Upon a wheel of fire, that mine own tears
> Do scald like molten lead.
>
> WILLIAM SHAKESPEARE, *King Lear*

"Cre-mate me! And put the ashes in a coffee can."

Dad was sitting in the rattan peacock chair in his living room, his eyes at half-mast, his head rolling side to side, as if moving to the beat of a seasick giraffe. He had decided that haircuts were too expensive, so his long, gray hair was pulled back in a ponytail. His cheekbones stuck out of his thin face. But he lit up with joy when he talked about his crematorium. So cheap! High on the morphine that floated him above his pain—"I'm swayin' in the breeze," he said—he shoved a piece of paper at me. In pencil, he had scrawled the name of his favorite cut-rate crematorium. His nurse had penned in the address.

"You go there," he said. He let his hand fall to his knee, which I knew he intended to slap. "I said, you give me the name of the ab-so-lute cheapest crematorium in New York City, and that's it!" His face shone with pride.

It was the Fourth of July, 1991. I couldn't get across town to the pharmacy with the morphine, because of the parade. On July 3, the day before he died, Dad had asked Mom if she visited her parents' graves, and she'd asked, "Why would I do that?"

"Did you know my mamma was born on the Fourth of July?" he'd answered. He was happy that I'd finally finished graduate school, at thirty.

Dad's rasping, irregular groans filled the room. My mother was sitting on the edge of her chair. Dad wanted for her to be there. My brother came in with a bottle of Mazola corn oil, anointed Dad, and prayed. A few days earlier when Roland had done this, he and Dad had been sitting up, smiling. But now Dad lay still, his eyes closed. As Roland dipped his finger in the corn oil and drew a cross on Dad's forehead, Mom stage-whispered, "X marks the spot!" Dad didn't react. Roland ran out of the apartment, though I begged him to stay.

By afternoon that day, Dad's eyes appeared to have marbles under the lids. His legs were swollen, his ankles purple. I thought he could no longer hear. I was looking for words, and my dry mouth couldn't seem to produce them. The phone rang. The doctor's voice boomed through the speakerphone. Suddenly, Dad yelled, "Kill me! Give me in-jec-tion!"

No, there was nothing we could give him, the doctor told me. No morphine injection. Too much morphine stops breathing. The doctor added, "He just doesn't want to go through it."

I got through the parade, finally, to the pharmacy on the East Side. I still had the refillable prescription. The bottle of yellow pills. I poured them into a bowl, crushed them, put in sugar and water. I told Dad I was doing this. He smiled. I painted the mixture inside his mouth.

I was the only one wearing black. Elderly sisters with broad-brimmed hats and tatted lace gloves shook my hand. Everybody cried but Mom, who seemed to drop lipsticks and break glasses with every move.

"I'm so sorry," she said, whirling around and stepping on another foot. That night, she couldn't sleep, so neither could

I, in the hotel room we were sharing in Dad's North Carolina hometown. I kept waking to the sound of Mom putting her toiletries in different baggies, the filled baggies falling to the bathroom floor, and Mom starting all over again.

The family headstone stretched like a limousine. Carved garlands graced its borders. Engraved across its pink granite expanse swirled the message A DAY OF DUTY DONE, A NIGHT OF REST BEGUN.

My day of duty was done: I did not have to kill Dad at the moment. My night of rest had not begun. Dad's sister let on that my grandfather expired during a carnal encounter after a large Thanksgiving dinner. She chuckled.

"At the penultimate moment, Mamma said."

"I can think of no better way to die."

I looked around the trimmed lawn of the cemetery, at the monument in polished rose granite under which Dad's ashes would rest.

"I love your mamma," he'd said to me the day before the morphine. "But you make me feel calm."

Then he'd clutched my hand and wouldn't let go.

On the morning of the day that I had to go pick up my father's ashes, Josef hugged me good-bye in my living room. I had been daydreaming about him for months before his visit. Three or four times a day, I got so sweaty with desire that I ducked into bathrooms at work, or my bedroom at home. I knew for sure as he hugged me that he loved me, too—also that I would never see him again. Just to see me, he had flown from Los Angeles to New York. I wanted nothing more than to fall into his arms. But I had not done so during our all-too-brief visit.

Dr. Sternbach had told me not to. I tried to obey his instructions, although I always felt scared that I was getting them wrong.

"Don't kiss him!"

I lay on the couch, wringing my hands. I heard an impatient sigh.

"I won't do anything. I won't hold hands or anything." The moment I said that, I felt that at least I could hold hands.

"You think about nothing but sex! You're a whore! He'll know you want sex."

"No, I won't. We'll just visit."

"*Ach,* you will ruin everything because you want sex."

"No, I won't."

"He will never marry you if you have sex with him."

"I've been afraid to tell you that I want sex with him because I am in love and dream about him all the time."

"You are not in love! When you are, I will be able to tell by the tip of your nose!" My analyst had told me he was always right. He thumped the end of the couch, near my head, and I knew to be quiet.

I did not want to hear his usual warning: "Besides, there's no sign that this man loves you."

During Josef's visit to New York, I toed the line, except for the moments when, walking through the Cloisters and the surrounding park, we held hands. Until I dropped his hand, I thought I was jeopardizing my chances of marrying him.

Right before he left, he hugged me good-bye and sighed. Now he was gone for good.

I did not want to pick up Dad's ashes alone. Right across the street from me lived Simon, an art dealer who kept kiddie porn under his bed.

Simon had a cultivated voice and the sadness of Dracula. It was hard to imagine love coming out of Simon or heading toward him. A few months earlier, I'd attended one of his soirées, where call girls and marginal artists flitted about in dim light filtered through Tiffany stained-glass lamps, admiring his extensive art collection and listening to opera singers tackle morbid death scenes. Portraits in ornate gold frames, Roman sculptures, mahogany gargoyles, enhanced the décor. Simon's large collection of Pre-Raphaelite damsels looked palely out of the wall as though he'd slept with them and never phoned them again.

After the front door closed behind the man with whom I'd wanted to spend my life, I heard the elevator move and knew he wasn't pushing the button, where I could still call to him, but riding down to the lobby. I lay down on the living room sofa. Josef was on the sidewalk now in his curly hair and red-and-purple shirt; he was hailing a cab, he was swinging his suitcase into the trunk, he was climbing in, shutting the cab door, the cab was speeding toward JFK Airport. I pictured him sitting in the cab, I saw him boarding the plane.

The night before, we had watched a German comedy about a man so in love with his estranged wife that when his roommate brings her home as his blind date, the husband grabs the nearest disguise—a King Kong mask and boxing gloves.

I picked up the phone to ask Simon to meet me at my father's apartment.

"Simon, it's me. I have an odd request."

"I love odd requests."

"Remember I told you my father was dying? Well, he's dead."

"I'll be there in ten minutes. I have an odd request myself."

I took a cab to Dad's house, let myself in, and started shoving leftover medicine bottles into a plastic bag.

Simon rang the intercom loudly, impatiently, and bounded in the door, which I'd left ajar.

When I greeted Simon, his rapacious expression, shock of thick, white hair, hawk nose, and knowing, mean-spirited chuckle pushed the memory of Dad's face into some hermetically sealed vault in my mind.

Without saying hello, Simon pulled me over to Dad's couch, hauled me onto his lap. I thought of my father's hands and feet turning blue as he gasped for air on the last day of his life. I wanted to seal off that memory, too.

"I would love to have you just once," Simon breathed into my ear, and suddenly this was what I craved. He turned me to face him, his large, eager eyes bearing down on mine.

"You look like a Roman emperor," I said.

"Which one? Nero?" He pulled me toward him. "So, Daddy died."

He pushed me down on the couch.

"Just put your hand here," he added, placing it on his crotch. He sniffed my neck.

Here was a way to feel nothing, at least nothing but sensation. I knew I could never long for him to love me.

"Shhh, girlie, you are trembling," he said. He sat back, looked me over, cocked his head as though he found the idea of me trembling a pleasure.

I got up, paced the length of the room. "I killed him. I did kill my father," I said.

Simon sat and stared at me with even more obvious desire. Then he laughed. "What are you talking about, you killed him? He was at death's door."

I edged toward the window and then turned to face Simon. Dad's living room was filled with light. The plants were very green.

Simon cackled and raised his voice, chanting, "She was a bad girl!" He adopted a mock-earnest expression, like the guy whirling the rattan cane in a porn video. "Come here, take your pants down, I'll spank you." He leaned forward and made a grab for me.

"Not now, Simon." I started watering the plants.

He looked at me quizzically. "I thought you'd be the type to enjoy that." He shrugged, crossed his legs. When he leaned forward, I saw that the inside of his shirt collar looked like the "before" sequence of a laundry detergent commercial.

"I was trying to tell you I killed my father."

"Aw, come on." He shook his head as if I were making a bad joke.

"He made me. He was screaming for a morphine injection."

"He made you?" Simon laughed again. "You fascinate me. Do you know, you're glamorous, for a newly minted PhD. I believe you. What happened, you got sick of emptying bedpans? I want a blow-by-blow. If you really killed him, that took guts."

I burst into tears, shrieked with laughter.

"My God, I thought you were kidding." He sat up straight, shook his head slowly, stretched his fingers, and rested them on the lapels of his jacket. "It's all right. It is. So you played the angel of death. Lots of daughters do." His fingers drummed his lapel, and then he let them drop into his lap.

"He yelled that I should kill him."

"So you injected him?" Simon inclined his head, as if awaiting instructions.

"No. I took the morphine pills and crushed them and mixed them with sugar and water and told him that I would spread them around his mouth, and I did."

"I can imagine that," Simon said, nodding slowly, as though he had actually done it himself and could give me some tips for next time. "Were you thinking that you loved him or that you hated him?"

"I was thinking that it had to be me, because my mother would have enjoyed it. He needed me. I gave him an overdose because he would not let go of my hand when he asked."

Simon got up. He had noticed Dad's blue-and-white Canton china candlesticks in the corner cupboard.

"Listen, dear, these are worth something." He removed them with the arrogance of Genghis Khan annexing a province. When I thought he was going to slide them into his pocket, he set them back.

Five Chinese ivory statues stood on a shelf above the candlesticks. He reached for the one that had been Dad's favorite, an elegant woman with a quiet smile, a baby on her back, grinning as the child tugs at the parasol she is holding. He ran his finger lightly, sensuously, over the ivory and peered at the statue's face in a way that made my flesh crawl.

Simon spoke again, but I couldn't make sense of his words.

"Listen to me!" Simon barked. "This one, the lady with the kid, this one needs mineral oil. Do it carefully, with a Q-tip. I can show you." He seemed a drill sergeant dispensing orders.

"Wrap this up, quick, before the estate appraiser gets here." Simon's voice jolted me. He grabbed a leftover box of adult diapers. "These'll do."

"Simon, Dad told me about mineral-oiling the ivories."

"So Daddy was an aesthete." Simon smirked. His long, bony fingers slid over baseboards, opened drawers. He squinted at vases like a jeweler hovering over the Hope Diamond.

Simon and I took a cab to the mortuary and zoomed up Broadway, then crosstown, and I watched the Upper West Side fall away. The cab stopped on a street littered with broken glass in front of a sign: "Domingo Funeraria."

We sat on folding chairs in the tiny foyer of the mortuary. Simon reached down, retied his Nikes, hugged me closer. I had a hunch that if a crack dealer were to rampage through waving a semiautomatic, Simon would use me as a human shield.

"Dad told me he wanted the cheapest—I told you he meant it."

"You did not exaggerate," Simon said. He rubbed the edge of my thigh and left his hand on it. A bemused professorial type in tortoiseshell glasses sat to our right. Crammed in on the other side was a large, hysterically sobbing Hispanic woman. Behind us, a voice yelled, "*Vamos!* Get up, bringing a body through!"

We jumped up, and two guys ran in carrying a black body bag that sagged heavily. The chapel door opened for a moment, and I caught a glimpse of flowers and a Plasticine Madonna. The Hispanic woman burst into loud weeping and followed the body bag into the chapel.

"Jesus!" Simon yelped. He gripped my thigh so hard it hurt, and I pried his hand off.

A woman holding a list entered the waiting area, called my name as if she were a nurse and I was the next patient in line. She handed me something the size of a shoebox wrapped in brown paper. It was heavier than it looked. I sat back down next to Simon and put the box of Dad on my lap.

Simon reared back in his seat, eyes widening.

I turned toward Simon, who seemed to be trying to lean further away, though he had no room to do so.

"Simon, this is my father." Black magic marker spelled out, on the side of the brown paper covering the box, the words HARRY KNOX CREMAINS. I thumped, heard a dull thud, and held the box up for Simon to see. His eyebrows shot up toward his hairline.

I turned to the woman who had handed me the box. "May I have a bag, please?"

Simon giggled. The young guy behind the desk said, "We don't have bags, but if you hold on, I'll get you one." I watched him sprint across the street. He came back breathing hard, handed me a plastic bag from the bodega. The bag had a picture of a man in a large sombrero surrounded by hunks of Swiss cheese and piles of ham. "El Guapo Food Warehouse" captioned his mustachioed face.

"My God!" Simon stage-whispered. "Can't you get him a bag from Zabar's?" He tugged at my sleeve, his eyes wild.

"We can't go. I have to get the death certificate."

Up a flight of creaking stairs we crept. At the top in a tiny office, a man who looked like Telly Savalas yelled into two phones at once as we stood in the doorway. "I told you! I need that car!" he screamed into one phone, then into the other, "It was drug related. Get that body outta there." He waved us toward him and pointed to a single straight-backed wooden chair. I sat, Simon's hands on my shoulders.

"Name?" the bald man barked.

I hadn't spoken Dad's name since he'd died. When I did, I started to cry. Simon's hands cupped my shoulders, and I thought I would cry more, but he just shook me a little, and I snapped out of it.

"Date of birth?" Baldie kept going, like the wheezing air conditioner in the corner of his office.

"Nineteen thirteen. June. I think."

"Cause of death?"

"Lung cancer."

"Age at death?"

"Uh, seventy-eight. Or nine."

"Name of deceased's mother?"

I told him.

"Name of deceased's father?"

Suddenly I was failing the exam. "I think it was James. I don't think I can remember. Does it matter?"

Behind me, Simon breathed, "It's all semantics." He stroked my hair.

The bald guy scribbled something and slapped a form down. "Sign here, sign here, sign here," he said, pointing to blank spaces that required my signature. "So how many death certificates ya need, fifteen bucks apiece?"

"I don't know. I thought I needed one."

The man's look of impatience deepened. "The bank. The will. Ya gotta think."

"She'll need five," Simon said, as if he ordered death certificates every day.

"I didn't bring cash. May I pay by credit card?"

"Nah, write me a check, 'cause I gotta pay two percent on the credit card."

"I don't have my—"

Simon pulled out his wallet.

"Allow me," he said in his best maître d' manner and plopped the cash down with a flourish. "I'll take care of you," he said, lifting an eyebrow. Through a blur of tears, I saw the man throwing his hands up, heard him mutter, "Shit. I don't have time," while both phones rang.

Simon kept his arm around me, telling the man, "Don't be a prick."

Smiling at the sight of the cash, Baldie pocketed it.

In the cab, Simon told me that when he had been in his thirties, he'd read all ten volumes of Havelock Ellis.

"Why?"

"I wanted to see if I had any of the perversions that he wrote about. I read every single case history, but he just never got to anything that seemed like me."

At Simon's building, the doorman looked at me sadly. He looked at Simon as if he wanted to say something but did not dare.

I left Dad's box of ashes on Simon's dining room table next to the electric dancing Coca-Cola can. When I pushed a button on the bottom of the can, it swayed from side to side with mechanical regularity. I turned it on and off a few times.

Simon came up behind me, put an arm around my waist, lifted my hair, licked my neck. "I can make you come more times than you can count," he said, and chuckled when I moaned.

I picked up the dancing Coke can and followed him up the stairs.

Simon's room was all bed. It was a from-here-to-eternity bed, a bed with intentions. Simon sat on the end, pulling me between his legs. I wished he would look at my face. When he did, I looked away. His hands rubbed slowly. I felt his lips, too eager. He grabbed my hips. I pushed him away.

"Oh, you want me to kiss you," he said. He touched and talked inventively, willing to do anything I liked, but I couldn't come.

Simon took my face in his hands, kissed my forehead, looked longingly, almost lovingly. Then I really couldn't come.

I pushed Simon's hands away and pretended I was alone. I did it myself, fantasizing girls being beaten, and he went wild when I came, but I put my back to him and looked at the Coca-Cola can. I turned it on, watched it weave from side to side, on and on, with no change, no purpose, and no place to go, forever.

TWENTY-TWO

The Exhibitionist

> Getting people right is not what living is all about
> anyway. It's getting them wrong that is living,
> getting them wrong and wrong and wrong
> and then, on careful reconsideration,
> getting them wrong again.
>
> PHILIP ROTH, *American Pastoral*

When I was in my late thirties, not long after my father's death, I phoned one of his former piano students to ask what he remembered of my family. Don, a nervous, shy man of manic garrulity, was willing to answer questions.

Don knew that I wanted to understand my father. We met at a dim café on the Upper West Side. As he approached my table, I glanced up at him and vaguely remembered a much younger, slimmer version of his face. I'd probably last seen him when I was in first grade. He looked embarrassed.

"You were about five." He stopped for a sip of coffee, and I was glad I'd swallowed mine before he went on. I would have choked.

"Your father was a very formal man, and he introduced you in a very stiff way. I remember he took me down the hall to meet you, and he said, 'This is my daughter, Melissa.' And you immediately pulled down your panties and said, 'And this is my vagina.'"

I gasped.

"You were a *little* girl," Don said. "Remember, just about five. I didn't look, because I felt embarrassed for him, and I was thinking what he must be feeling. So I never got a good look." Don giggled.

I sat across from him in the noisy, crowded café, thinking Sternbach was right about everything whenever he screamed that I was "an exhibitionist!"

I had dim memories of myself, age five, rushing in naked to some luncheon my mother was hosting. "I see London! I see France! I see Mommy's underpants!" I'd screeched, conscious of having none on myself.

I don't know how old I was, but I was old enough to remember—too far along in childhood to have been doing such things. I wasn't two. But five? Might have been six? Only a *very* disturbed child would disrobe in public, I felt sure.

When I'd been about that age, Dad had ordered the whole family to take a stroll on Riverside Drive one afternoon, announcing loudly, the minute we'd passed our doorman, and as the winds billowed out my mother's skirts, which she seemed to be patting down, "Mamma don't have any underpants on!"

Mom, my brother, and I had reddened, but we kept walking.

"Your father was such a formal man," Don repeated, shrugging. "I felt for him, really."

After I left the café and as I walked down Broadway, I thought about Dad sweeping me and my brother into the bathroom, hooting, "Watch Daddy pee."

Maybe I had thought, *When you introduce someone, you say hello and then you display your wares.*

Or maybe I was a sick weirdo, as Sternbach said.

I remembered the time he'd looked at my class photo, said I wanted to be stared at—he tapped the photo, disapproving of my Peruvian sweater. I put that sweater away and didn't take it out of storage or wear it again until years later, when I finally shook it out, tried it on again, and felt my old delight at the perky white llamas walking across the middle.

By my third year in college, I'd relinquished another symptom of my exhibitionism: dance classes. Sternbach's demands that I give them up had less impact than his insistence that dance was a symptom. My narcissism and exhibitionism remained, he said, significant problems interfering with my ability to meet men. I wasn't meeting men, and I could blame no one but myself. Or I met them, but as soon as I exhibited the details of my adventures with them to Sternbach, things never worked out.

Soon after my meeting with Don, I arranged a date with a man whom I found very attractive, although I suspected we had too little in common. A successful businessman, he squired me around to lovely Greek restaurants and trendy bars. One night, he'd started kissing me at a bar table, and I'd let him bring me home, where we kissed and touched a long time. Suddenly he climbed on top and tried to force sex, and I threw him off. If he'd been taller and weighed more, I might not have been able to fight him. He'd have raped me, no doubt.

I had to tell Dr. Sternbach, who had just gotten back from vacation, about my fiasco of a date—that I'd felt "so aroused"—and Sternbach said, "You don't even know how terrible that sounds" and told me if I behaved like this, I would always meet men who would treat me like "a street girl," and that if I wanted to see the man again, I should absolutely not have any sex. He was so angry as I was telling the story that he kept interrupting me and I couldn't even tell it, as in,

"... and then we had our hands in each others' genitals, and—"

"How could you *do* that? What were you *thinking*? You're not a little girl! You are an adult, a thirty-seven-year-old woman, right?"

"Well, I'm forty, actually."

"So I'm a nice guy."

"Welcome home from vacation."

"In spite of what I told you, you do it anyway . . . oh, you do treatment for years and years," he muttered to himself, dispiritedly. He shot an angry look at me. "You are like a cat in heat."

"I want a family—I really do want children."

"It's too late!"

"Are you going to help me?"

"Are you going to shoot me?"

I was well aware of turning forty and having nothing that I wanted—a husband whom I loved, and children—but Dr. Sternbach told me that I did not want children, had no interest in raising them, and was "too difficult" to be attractive to most men. I figured, at this point, that a little sex was better than no romance. I figured I had lost the love of my life anyway, so that nothing mattered much anymore. All my problems, I had no doubt, were my fault. Dr. Sternbach tried so hard to help me.

I was forty when Sternbach announced his retirement one week before he closed up shop. His psychiatrist daughter, he told our stunned group, thought he should quit.

In our final session a few days later, he told me I was "cold," that I had "no warmth" and "a psychotic core."

"Your *mother* is warm!" he said. "You, not. Look what she did for you! She paid for college and analysis! Anybody could be proud to have a mother like yours! Your mother is *giving*! You are not." He had said this recently in one of the last group meetings, and everyone had nodded seriously in agreement.

I lay on the couch weeping, because now that he was retiring, I would have no guidance.

"You are thinking of my death," he said. "And I will die. I am old."

"I don't know how I'll function without you." I felt completely convinced that I had no judgment—he had told me so—and needed him to explain things to me.

He shrugged. "You will go through a mourning period, like everybody else. Being old is bad, I always say, but consider the alternative."

I laughed.

"Age is also a time when you grow. I am much less inhibited, even in my dreams," he began. "The other night I had a dream I could never have had when I was young. You know my sister, the one who died in the Warsaw ghetto."

Yes, I did.

"I dreamed I was lying in bed and then my sister climbed in beside me, naked. She reached out to me. It then occurred to me that in addition to being a beautiful woman, she was my sister. But I thought, so *what?*" He laughed.

"And then what happened?"

"As I reached for her, I woke up!" He slapped his thighs with merriment. "You see the dreams of an old man?"

"I don't know what I will do without you," I said. "You make me laugh."

"Here is a psychoanalytic joke!" he smiled.

I sat up on the couch and turned to look at him. He was smiling, reclined in his chair.

"A man went to his psychoanalyst with a dream. In the dream, he's rowing on a lake, but his paddles keep getting close to rocks and whirlpools, and the paddles will break and the boat will crash, and just at this minute, the man wakes up. He goes to his analyst and tells him the dream, and the analyst interprets: 'You're dreaming about sex, but this is an oedipal dream, incestuous sex, so you are punishing yourself by destroying the paddles—phallic symbols—on the rocks.'

"The man goes home and returns next session with another dream. 'I'm lying in bed naked,' he says, 'and my mother comes in and takes off her clothes and climbs into bed with me. Then I wake up.' His analyst says, 'So what do you think this means?' The man says, 'That's easy. It means I want to go rowing.'"

Dr. Sternbach and I laughed, and then I cried, thinking I'd never have a companion as interesting as he. I knew I pleased him by listening to him and finding him amusing, and when I pleased him, I felt deeply fulfilled—for a few minutes. Then I went right back to being terribly sad, depressed, and hopeless. I was certain the cure lay in spending more time with Dr. Sternbach.

"Never mind," he said in his kind voice. "You can come vacation with us to Bad Ragaz." He and his wife would be staying at a five-star hotel with famous thermal baths in an alpine region of Switzerland.

At least I wouldn't have to forge ahead without Sternbach—not yet.

I booked a room with a hot plate and shared bath at the cheapest place I could find within walking distance of their hotel. Haus Romantica, populated by quiet students, was a misnomer, I wrote in my journal. Sniffing the ancient, musty timbers and the sheets that had lain on a shelf too long, I wrote, "I'd call it Haus Mildewica."

Every day I met the Sternbachs, either for a meal or a drink. At one point, I asked if I could contribute, because they always paid. Taking a lock of my hair and yanking it, Sternbach replied, "Contribute your smile."

I took long walks, alone, on the grounds and went to a nearby geological formation called the Taminaschlucht, a narrow gorge that could be walked through, with waters—source of the local spa—rushing through at speeds faster than a kayak could maneuver. The uneven stone edges of the gorge soared jaggedly above me like a vault designed to immure a prisoner, probably for life, but a little sky shone through at the very top. I walked the length of the thing with the sound of rushing waters echoing off the dripping walls and emerged again into bright sun, meadows, and alpine flowers.

Then it was back to the Haus Romantica, where I spent moments not passed with the Sternbachs. I was lying in bed one afternoon trying to read *Adventures of Huckleberry Finn* when someone knocked loudly on the outer door.

I leaped out of bed. I did have a Swiss friend, a college professor, a trailblazer in his numbers-and-science-filled field, an expert practitioner in an area of academics I understood not at all. I knew he was planning to take the train from Bern to spend a day with me. I'd toyed with the idea of turning my amiably flirtatious, conversational friendship with this man into an affair, and I wondered if it might be he banging on my door in such an urgent fashion. Maybe he'd decided to show up early, surprise me. Maybe he was even now standing outside in hiking boots and a Tyrolean hat, carried away by passion.

He'd picked me up at the airport in Zurich, taken me to dinner, and kissed me goodnight in a teasingly chaste manner. His merry eyes, craggy face, shock of blond hair perpetually falling over his forehead, and tall, wiry frame all appealed to me.

I ran a brush through my hair, dabbed on lipstick, and went to the door.

There stood Mrs. Sternbach, an anxious, respectful look on her worn face. A few feet behind, probably because he did not want to climb the slightly upward slope to the Haus Romantica, Oscar Sternbach stood leaning on a cane, a look of dread on his face.

"Are you all right?" he demanded.

"Yes," I said, puzzled. "I'm fine." We hadn't made any particular plans. I felt tired and dispirited and had wanted to spend an hour or two lying in bed.

"We did not hear from you!" he accused.

"Dr. Sternbach thought you might be ill," his wife said, moving back down the little hill and taking his elbow gently.

"No, I'm fine!" I said. We arranged to meet for dinner. I closed the door and lay back down with Huckleberry Finn, who, unlike me, had the sense to light out for the territories on his own.

The next morning, I met the Sternbachs in their room to discuss the day. He was sitting in a chair, so quiet I thought he might be falling asleep. His wife and I chatted for about five minutes, about the Fosamax she was taking, the best spas, restaurants in the area. Suddenly he yelled, "No one is thinking of *me*!" in a voice filled with outrage. A look of pain flashed across his wife's face.

I'd brought with me to Switzerland a toy New York yellow cab that I planned to give as a gift to the man whom I longed to see but dared not hope to be loved by: Josef.

When I gave Josef his taxi, he grinned, kissed me, and played with it. But I'm getting ahead of my story.

I'd emailed Josef that I was coming to Bad Ragaz with the Sternbachs and wondered if he might like to visit and go hiking. Hope springs eternal, and I wanted to see his face. It had been six years since we'd first met, and I'd thought of him often.

Josef emailed me that he'd love to come to Switzerland to see me.

When he knocked on the door one evening, I started to sweat even before I answered. There he was with his smiling blue eyes, his curly hair, and a big hug for me. He entered, ready for dinner, rice and chicken that I'd overcooked on the hot plate.

I apologized. "I don't know how that happened to the chicken!"

186

"Oh, probably cooking it at low heat for too long," he said, eating enthusiastically. He loved to solve my problems, I could see. He ate and drank with gusto.

My room had two narrow beds, one on each wall, and that first night, and the next night, and, it seems to me now, even the third night, we slept in our separate beds. Or rather, I lay awake watching his face, which seemed even sweeter as he slept. He met the Sternbachs, too: we had an outdoor café lunch. When Josef's beer came in a stein that must have seemed, by Bavarian standards, either stingy or miniature, I saw his face fall. He perked up when I mentioned that he could always order another.

On the following gorgeous day, we hiked through many trails, through that prisonlike gorge the Taminaschlucht, and found ourselves, in late afternoon, in the rain. A small B&B on the side of the road advertised a sauna.

Sauna. That lit me up. I'd recently discovered European saunas. What a contrast! Especially after the one in the Columbia University gym, where you lay on a dull plastic plank staring at a plastic ceiling, surrounded by other disillusioned women, and the temperature never rose above eighty-five degrees.

On my first day in Igls, Tyrol, a small town near Innsbruck, Austria, where I'd gone for a week of rest and relaxation before planning to meet the Sternbachs, I entered the sauna at the end of the women's locker room and stretched out on my towel. Clean, redolent of herbs, and considerably hotter than anything I'd experienced before, it was large, a room done in pine planks—walls, ceiling, benches—and lit in warm glows. I settled on a bench, luxuriating in the heat and the marvelous aromas of arnica and eucalyptus, amazed at how much nicer this place was than the grubby Columbia University sauna. Then the door opened. Before I opened my eyes, I heard a voice.

Male.

You entered the one and only sauna, I had not known, from either the men's or the women's dressing room.

I sat up. The handsome, naked, dark-haired Austrian said something in German, and I had no idea what it was. He did not sound as though he were saying he'd like to rape me. He seemed to be asking a question. I said I didn't speak German that well, and did he speak English?

"Oh, yes, I do," he said in a heavy accent. "I vas chust vondering wair you haf *das Wasser*. I mean, water."

I pointed to the bucket, and he poured it over the hot stones to make the sauna steamy. Then he sat down on his bench, closed his eyes, and relaxed, and I lay back on mine, less relaxed. Wow! A naked man! I could stare at him! What an American I was! Europeans weren't like me! They didn't have to stare—they got to see naked people all the time! I was so unsophisticated! Wow! A naked man! He could look at me, too. We could stare at each other if we weren't too obvious about it. All this was socially acceptable. How *fabulous*.

The scene came back to me as I stood in the cold rain with Josef, mud darkening our shoes.

We were both looking at the sauna sign.

Exhibitionism, here I come, I thought. We booked the afternoon in the sauna for some ridiculous fee like twelve American dollars and disrobed in front of each other, matter-of-factly and looking sideways. Josef lay in a deck chair and clowned around, flinging himself back so that the head of the thing hit the floor and his feet rose in the air.

"I'm going to squirt you with this water!" I threatened, aiming the hose at him.

"If you do, you will have to take the consequences," he said with a big grin.

I squirted. The consequences were great. They went on all afternoon, until, hungry, we staggered back to the Haus Romantica, where romance truly blossomed.

I wasn't out of Sternbach's clutches yet. But I was loosening his grip.

Sternbach said he would attend our wedding but didn't. When I was five months pregnant with our first child, Josef and I agreed to meet him, again in Switzerland, a seven-hour drive from our home in Bavaria. Dr. Sternbach rolled up in a wheelchair near the foot of the Jungfrau, just as I was expressing surprise at seeing Chassidic Jews pedaling up the mountainside.

"Those awful people, the Jews!" he declaimed, addressing my German husband. "Really, we should throw them out of here." He grinned expansively and regaled us with how he had, as an Austrian Jewish lawyer in 1938, gone through Adolf Eichmann's emigration office, Zentralstelle für jüdische Auswanderung, right after the Anschluss, leaving behind, he said, a girlfriend with whom he was never reunited and the sister who died in the Warsaw ghetto. Glancing again at my husband, Dr. Sternbach raised his arm in a Nazi salute. "*Heil* Hitler!" he yelled. Then he took his arm back down, but not for long. He turned to me with a confidential air, ignoring Josef, drawing closer to me in his wheelchair, and wagged a finger in my face like a schoolmaster.

"Always remember, your husband must be your *Führer. Sieg Heil!*" he announced, his arm jerking up at the elbow again, as if he were Hitler himself reviewing the troops. He looked pleased with himself.

Josef is an understanding man, but by this time, his face was a pale green, and he cast me a wounded glance before shrugging, grinning, and putting his arm around me so that we could face Dr. Sternbach together.

"Look, darling," Josef smiled, after the café *mit schlag,* after the good-byes, "I could have told him that my grandfather nearly got sent to Dachau because he wouldn't join the Nazis, or I could have invented a Satanic, cigar-chomping Heinrich Himmler. Don't you think your Dr. Sternbach would have loved me as much either way?"

The question thrust me back to the moment when I'd lain in tears on Sternbach's analytic couch, my ears ringing: "Listen to me! Doctor's orders! I already told you he'll never marry you! And of course it's too late for children."

It chilled me to think that I could have gone on believing in Sternbach for the rest of my life.

He lived long enough to meet my first child, who crawled up and anointed his feet with drool. The stricken look on Sternbach's face was sweet revenge, but I've never rid myself of him completely. That would take an exorcism.

TWENTY-THREE

Divorcing Mom

The land of spices; something understood.

GEORGE HERBERT, "Prayer"

I leave psychoanalysis as one leaves any religion—ambiva-
lently. The unconscious, the defenses, the drives, Eros and
Thanatos—these concepts furnish my thinking, such that I find
it hard to remove them when I wish to do so. You know how
certain sexual fantasies always work even if you think of them
as boring old dishrags?

The power of the analyst as the wiser party, the one who
helps the patient "work through" psychic issues—that's the atom
bomb. You have to be willing to blow yourself up to get psycho-
analyzed. The minute you stop asking, *what does my heart tell
me?* and start telling yourself, *I better listen to the analyst, who
knows best, is able to see my problems more clearly than I do,*
you're in trouble, even if the analyst can see your problems better.

Or especially. What I wanted and needed at age fourteen—to
escape from my mother and my family, to find another mother—
became the chief issue of a psychoanalysis bent on indoctrinating
me with the idea that "your mother will always help you!" the
way Sternbach would always help me. The longing to believe in
something overpowered any good sense I may have had. The

appeal of the idea of a God who had a definite answer merged in my mind with the notion that my mother, like Sternbach, wanted to protect me.

My mother paid—week after week, month after month, year after year.

At fourteen, I smelled a rat—but never trusted my hunches. If only Mom had summoned the sense to say, "Let's get out of this overbearing man's office!" But she behaved as she did when we got into a taxi to go to a dentist's or a doctor's appointment. Instead of firmly announcing the address to which she wanted to repair, she'd lean forward with a tragic look, as if begging the driver not to beat her. In a squeaky little-girl voice, she would say, "Please? To? Uh, driver, if you could? Take us? To . . . ?"

To The Eldorado, or to Dr. Berkeley, or to "Dr." Sternbach—wherever the gods advertised the possibility of salvation. I wanted her to know what to do, but the poor thing had no idea.

Every pore of Mom screams "I need a mommy," and no wonder. Trusting Dr. Berkeley to heal and marry her, Mom never saw how much the woman used her. She tossed my mother to Dad like a bone, abandoning her when Mom had served her purpose of producing offspring for Harry. Mom had money; Dad had none. She was a bargain. That's one impression I get from a letter Dr. Berkeley wrote to Dr. Sternbach when I first started treatment.

She discloses that Mom, newly arrived home from the hospital, my newborn brother in tow, had horrified her by showing me her shaved vulva and telling me that this was where my brother Roland came from.

I can imagine the scene. The young mother can't wait to be welcomed with joy by her two-year-old daughter, me, the only one around who likes her. Surely, the second Mom's little pal lays eyes on *Your new brother! A present all for you!!* she'll fall in love. But then the two-year-old acts like a two-year-old, declining even to cast a glance in the direction of this red-faced, screaming interloper, let alone the hag who's dared to bring him home. What's with this unnecessary baby? *Take him back,* I say. *Let's take the wee tiny baby brother back to the hospital.*

That must have been when Mom hoped that if she showed off the very best part of herself—the part her own father fondled, and it didn't bother her one bit, in fact, seemed so unimportant she never mentioned the activity to Aunt Berkeley—I'd like her again. I'd be grateful. I'd appreciate her. Finally.

So when I, at age five or six, took to startling dinner guests by announcing, "Look at my vagina!" (Upstager! Scene-stealer!) I wanted to be like Mom.

For an exhibitionist, I was pretty inhibited by the time I got to Sternbach. I hid behind a curtain of long hair and baggy tie-dye T-shirts. On my very first appointment, the momentary shock of seeing myself in that mirror behind his front door brought nothing but revulsion. I wanted, above all, to hide, to escape into another world.

But Sternbach found in me a mirror of his own wish—a young girl who would hang on his every word, unlike the mother who fired his wet nurse when he was an infant, he informed me, adding, "And this was very bad for me!" Unlike his sister, who left him by dying in the Warsaw ghetto. This, after she'd been weeping as they prepared to leave Vienna, the very last thing he said to the sister he'd never see again being, "What are *you* crying for? You get to stay in Europe! We have to go live with the barbarians!"

I was the repository of every thought, feeling, and desire he chose to exhibit: he told me of his marriages, his girlfriends, the kinds of contraceptives he'd used, why he found scented Ortho-Gynol gel disgusting, his theories of incest in the opera *Lohengrin,* his daughter's dislike of her own mother, her problems with heartbreak and boyfriends and marriage, his fears of aging and dying.

It proved a relief to read Dr. Berkeley's letter and to learn that what I had always sensed about my mother was real. Now I understood why I could hardly bear for Mom to touch me. I remembered, almost against my will, many instances when suddenly she'd be in the room without a top, or she'd be doing ballet stretches without underpants on. In the living room, where anyone could see her.

After years with Sternbach, I had become the exhibitionist who could never reveal her feelings. Mom had become someone whose side Aunt Berkeley never took, whose resentment spilled out onto me. I wasn't a good enough mommy for Mom.

Never realizing that she had not received salvation from Dr. Berkeley, Mom continues to wander in search of a mother she will never have, an approval that will never be bestowed. She regards Dr. Berkeley as the woman who "freed me from my childhood," never the woman who took advantage of her childish ways, had no sympathy for her, and ridiculed her.

I'm now a lapsed patient—more than twenty years clean and sober, able to hold conversations with members of the faith without imbibing in the practice myself. Sternbach's Holy Article of Faith, my mother's greatness, is the one I've desecrated, divorcing her for my sake as well as my family's.

Years ago, on a family trip to Nantucket, my mother sat next to my five-year-old daughter as we rode the bus to the beach. I sat across, a crowd of people jostling between us. My mother's arm around my daughter's shoulder seemed to be squeezing her too hard, and my daughter was gazing fixedly off in the opposite direction. Mom had on her face the smug look of a child getting away with something as her hand slipped down to my daughter's leg, which she grasped. Her face assumed a spacey look, she hummed, and her hand, as if operating on its own, rhythmically squeezed my daughter's thigh. Had Mom's thumb been a half-inch higher, penetration could have occurred.

"Would you like to come sit by me, sweetie?" I asked my daughter.

The bus slowed. My daughter got up and sat beside a woman with a baby, and played with the baby.

For the rest of the trip, I never left my daughter alone with my mother.

I wonder what my former therapists, or my mother's many friends, would think if they could have heard my thirteen-year-old son say, after that two-week summer holiday spent with her, "Gee, Mom. You grew up with *that*? You know, I kind of admire you." I'm pretty sure he doesn't remember my mother easing herself into a split in front of him when he was three years old. She wasn't wearing any underpants, and she wasn't wearing much on top either. Thank God for *Bob the Builder,* which he found more interesting. I ran and got a robe, hoping she wasn't "cold." Even then, I told myself she didn't realize what she was doing (probably true) and must mean well (probably not).

Whenever I'm asked how often I get to see my mother, who lives an ocean away from us, I tell the truth: only once or twice a year. People slap their hands to their cheeks in sympathy: "I know how much you must miss her!" or "This must be so hard for you! Your mother is so *great!*"

That's true—as long as you're not a member of her family. "Yes, I miss her tremendously," I lie. "But we're glad that we still have her!"

What I lack the courage to say is: I wish my mother would move to a remote planet, die there, and be buried by aliens so hostile to humanity that nobody would blame me for missing the funeral.

I remembered the angry face of Oscar Sternbach repeatedly insisting that Mom was "a wonderful mother." She would "do *anything* for you," he said, insisting that I had *no idea* what it was like to be a mother. He shook his fist.

At the time he was telling me these things, I was not yet a mother. He made motherhood sound like torture, especially with a child like me, who never appreciated Mom's suffering *and all she does for you*. He told me he saw no evidence that I wanted to be a mother.

"You just want a doll to play with, not a child! You don't want to watch a child grow! You don't want to *bring up* a child!"

I burst into tears and agreed. He must be right.

Another psychoanalyst, a nice, grandmotherly type whom I consulted because my mother had invited us on that Nantucket vacation, urged me to enjoy my time there and not to be anxious.

"Nothing can happen!" she smiled. If she'd seen it with her own eyes, would she have believed that scene on the bus?

Advising an "in one ear, out the other" policy around Mom's pronouncements, this analyst urged me to keep in contact with Mom.

"If this were any other old lady, I'd say fuck it! Get rid of her. But this is your mother, and you *do not want* that guilt."

How would a woman as sweet as this analyst—I gazed with wonder at Facebook photos of her tending a roast for her family—have a clue?

I'll take the guilt, Dr. Grandma.

I've always found myself alone in my feeling that the best way to handle Mom is to stay as far away from her as possible. Even Josef thinks she ought to be allowed "supervised" contact with the children. He thinks that as long as he and I are in the same room, nothing can happen.

One night, I left my husband supine on the sofa with the nightly news. A glass of wine in hand, I went upstairs to turn to the internet. I took a sip, Googled "difficult mother," and flipped through a few blogs and websites.

Around midnight, Daughters of Narcissistic Mothers popped up. The date was October 31, and I'd tricked around enough on the net to get my treat.

You are not to blame, said the website. You can go *no contact.* You can even *lie to her.*

I sipped wine and smiled. Lie to her! Why had it never occurred to me to do so?

When she says *I love you,* she means *I'd like to manipulate you.*

I drained my glass. Lie to her! Wow! This was better advice than I'd gotten from every shrink I'd consulted since Sternbach. Not even the better shrinks said, *Never see her again!*

They said, *You might notice your mother becoming more distant when you have children* or, *It's better not to tell her much about your life.*

I didn't have the guts for the gold standard of "no contact" that the Daughters of Narcissistic Mothers website presented. I'd settle for *limited* contact. Mom might after all leave us some money when she dies, I told myself, even though a thousand a month was going to my brother's former girlfriend, who seemed to be my mother's current girlfriend. Mom had money, and we needed our roof fixed. But it took the event on the bus with my daughter to make me realize that I could not rely on advice from therapists. I knew better.

So I send her chocolates and wine and I tell her how wonderful she is. Whenever she wants to see the kids, I make up any old excuse. I can avoid spending time with her, as long as I praise her.

To know that I can lie to her remains the greatest relief of my life. Like many divorced couples, we get along famously. I know what she wants to hear, and I say just that. As long as I reveal nothing about myself, we're both happy.

Epilogue

Alles hat ein Ende nur die Wurst hat zwei.

Everything has an end except a sausage, which has two.

GERMAN PROVERB

I remember a moment in Dr. Sternbach's psychotherapeutic group. His daughter, he told us, had had a birthday. Her husband had given her some jewelry.

"It was incredibly ugly jewelry," Dr. Sternbach remarked, shaking his head in astonishment.

He just could not believe how tasteless a piece of jewelry it was. But, he went on in even more disbelief, his daughter had exclaimed over it joyfully, covering her husband with gratitude and kisses.

Dr. Sternbach touched his hand to his chest, shaking his head, filled with disgust for the poor taste of his son-in-law.

"I know my daughter well!" he told us, nodding, and he felt sure that she could not possibly have liked such a thoroughly pathetic piece of non-art.

The gift was so bulky, so non-*Wiener-Werkstätte,* so unforgivably modern, so tackily American, that she must have been *acting,* she could only have been *pretending,* when she put on that show of gratitude, and actually, Dr. Sternbach remarked, forefinger waving, he approved of that! A woman should always pretend to love any present given to her by her husband. He went on at length about that, about virtue, about submissiveness.

Finally, one of the men in the group—the women would not have dared—said, "Come *on,* Dr. Sternbach."

Sternbach laughed. He pointed to each one of us in turn: "*You* have an Oedipus complex. And *you* have an Oedipus complex. And *you* have an Oedipus complex . . . but I"—here he gestured with a "who me?" expression worthy of Miss Piggy—"*I* don't have any Oedipus complex at all!"

But he once told me that his own analyst had insisted he was "hanging on" to his daughter—who lived and practiced psychiatry in the same building and had a gigantic portrait of him over the marital bed. This I heard from her husband.

And how did I know her husband? Because he's a pulmonologist, and Dr. Sternbach selected him to treat my father for lung cancer.

Oedipus, shmedipus. As long as you love your analyst.

Freud could have used my case in his 1907 article "Obsessive Acts and Religious Practices," which details the ways in which religious rituals fend off guilty feelings. Like a nun telling her beads, I chanted, "Dr. Sternbach is always right!" as I walked toward his building. Or I said to myself, *I'm an idiot,* because I hadn't liked something he'd said.

When I was twenty-two, I was already imagining my Jewish refugee analyst as a Nazi sadist: "With Herr Doktor: follow advice on faith and groan or grin and bear it." I hardly dared to speak thoughts that forced their way in, but I did pour them into journals.

I didn't want to believe the obvious. I thought what I had accurately diagnosed about him just could not possibly be true. I pushed the thought out of my head as much as I could.

I had of course heard from a number of friends and acquaintances about a different kind of therapist, the kind that encouraged "clients"—I was so used to hearing "patients"—to say what was on their minds. These other therapists, I was told, just kept asking questions, and were "nonjudgmental."

For Dr. Sternbach, such noninterventionist listening meant wandering in the desert without Moses's all-important pillar of fire by night or pillar of cloud by day.

Once I told Sternbach a story of a forum at a local college in which a psychologist discussed a young woman she'd seen who was suffering in law school. After a few sessions, the unhappy law student said she had always wanted to be an artist but her father had insisted that she go to law school. The story ended with the girl leaving law school, starting art school, and enjoying an improved mood. She had developed insights into her own condition, the psychologist said, and these insights enabled her to make the right decision.

Wham! Fist on couch.

Sternbach ranted, yelling so hard I had difficulty finishing the story. The word "insight" rendered him apoplectic. The therapist, he let me know, was "an idiot"—she should have helped the girl stick to her guns and finish law school. Not float around in useless "insights." What did a kid know? Nothing. He snapped his fingers. The law student needed guidance, not insights. That therapist had deprived the girl of a feeling of achievement. Too many therapists were loosey-goosey permissive; they did not strengthen people but let them regress. When friends mentioned what *their* therapists said, I laughed. Or felt smug. Dr. Sternbach and I, we knew better, didn't we? Insight was for wimps. "Suggestion," he said, was therapy. When he told me to do so, I signed up for graduate school, wishing I could go to dance class and remembering how I'd enjoyed acting in plays in college.

"Everybody," Dr. Sternbach lectured, thought Freud had given up suggestion as part of therapy, and everybody, Sternbach insisted, "was wrong." These fools with their "insight" were frauds, this therapist letting a patient leave law school for art school a disaster.

Freud's biographers will tell you that he discarded direct suggestion. He stopped doing hypnosis, right?

But he absolutely "did not give up suggestion," said Dr. Sternbach: you could read in Freud's last paper, "Constructions in Analysis," that he practiced *direct* suggestion as part of a legitimate psychoanalysis. It says so, in Strachey's *Standard Edition,* right on page 260 of vol. XXIII, that the analyst "finishes a piece of construction and communicates it to the subject of the analysis so that it *may work upon him.*"

Dr. Sternbach believed that last phrase was intended as a medicinal dose to chemically convert the patient to the analyst's "construction" of events.

To this day, I have not told Hannah what I now think of our so-called therapy. When I phoned her in the winter of 2015, I asked what she remembered of Dr. Sternbach.

"He was just the most interesting man I'd ever talked to," she said, adding, "Oh, Melissa, I had boyfriends. But *he* was the man in my life."

I visited her in April 2016. An old lady now, memory failing, she still wore the lovely turquoise Navajo ring with the oval stone that I remembered so well, and when I asked her to let me look at some of the journals she had kept about the group, she gave the go-ahead, suggesting I read out loud. I opened a volume and did so, learning she wept in Dr. Sternbach's office because when she asked what to do when her boyfriend wasn't nice, Sternbach told her to force the boyfriend to buy her something—a boutique or at least a TV.

"Dr. Sternbach is more like a lawyer than a helping professional," she wrote. "I cried when I told him that."

On many a page, she expressed a wish to leave Sternbach and the group.

That's when he called her a "ballbreaker."

She recorded my twenty-eighth birthday in the group, for which she had baked brownies, and the way Dr. Sternbach flirted with me, and how jealous she felt.

"Don't read more," she said gently. "You might find something you don't like."

Despite my reassurances, she was adamant that I stop reading. By the next day, when I called her, she had forgotten our visit.

In that golden shrine, The Eldorado, where I had at age fifteen wandered through the Wechsler–Bellevue Intelligence Scale, the Rorschach, the Thematic Apperception Test, the Human Figure Drawing and Bender Gestalt tests—garnering abysmal marks—resided, among all the lesser psychoanalysts and clinical psychologists, that holy grail of Freudians Dr. Kurt R. Eissler, who reportedly numbered among his analysands Jacqueline Kennedy Onassis.

I felt thrilled when I actually met the gaunt, stooped Dr. Eissler. For an entire afternoon, I worked for him in a secretarial capacity, hoping to ask him something about the Freud archives, namely, letters, tapes, secrets—cocooned on restricted shelves—in the Library of Congress. These archives overflow with compromising information about Freud, his followers, and their patients.

When I went to work for Eissler, I already knew the tragic story everybody was talking about, that the Oedipus complex, the rock on which the entire Freudian edifice stood and upon which my "therapy" had been erected, had been hacked at by a young psychoanalyst to whom the aging Eissler had given his absolute trust. Eissler had also given this guy complete access to these restricted archives. Not only that—Eissler had regarded the young psychoanalyst, Jeffrey Masson, not as a colleague but as a son, before ultimately shunning him as a traitor. Oh, the upstart son slaying his aging father's dreams! Oh, the oedipal drama!

Masson's enthusiasm had melted the shy Eissler's loneliness with a handshake that was almost a kiss. Like the queen who promises to hand over her firstborn to Rumpelstiltskin, the elderly Eissler imagined that nobody would really take away that baby. Masson, however, dumped out the baby, bathwater and all. Diving into those forbidden archives, the only human being allowed to see them, apart from Eissler, Masson read, Masson revealed, and Masson published the notion that Freud had lied—to himself and others. He had lied about sexual abuse. Lack of moral courage led Freud to believe that children mostly fantasized sexual seductions and attacks. The attacks really happened, Masson said, and the Freudians, refusing to recognize their reality, said children fantasized them as part of the development of the Oedipus complex.

Masson's ideas made sense to me, knowing, as I did, that my father really had fondled me and feeling that I could not be considered the one who seduced him, even if I had liked his

201

behavior, which occasionally, I dimly recall, I did, while feeling at the same time scared, guilty, and sure that I was not allowed to say "no" or "stop." If I had said either, neither of us would have loved me.

Eissler fired Masson, so Masson sued.

Over aromatic goat cheese and organic California mesclun, at Berkeley's hottest restaurant, Chez Panisse, the journalist whom the *New Yorker* had chosen to investigate the story, Janet Malcolm, daughter of a psychiatrist, author of a book on photography, and eager to defend her father and the profession, failed to inspire Jeffrey Masson to seduce her.

Or so I surmise. In her article, Malcolm described Masson as an "intellectual gigolo," so he sued her, too.

The story broiled on, in the *New Yorker,* the *New York Times,* the nightly news, but I accepted Sternbach's idea that I'd be wasting time reading any of it. I accepted even the intimation that the story was not for little girls. Then I read Malcolm and confessed, with fear, that I had done so.

"*Ach!*" he groaned. "This woman is a *Mieskeit,*" using a Yiddish word that means "ugly little woman."

When I got home, I looked at the photo of Malcolm on the cover of her book and convinced myself that she looked ugly. Though it seemed to me she looked thoughtful, intellectual, and attractive, I told myself I was wrong.

Never mind that Eissler's star rose high enough for the *New Yorker.* Never mind what anyone said outside the world of Sternbach's office.

There I was, in my thirties, miserably alone, seeking salvation in the office of yet another old man.

I guess I wanted to emerge from my Eissler encounter with the equivalent of a Zen koan communicating the notion that I was right about my father's drunken fumblings and that Sternbach, who insisted I had seduced Dad, was also right. If I believed these contradictory things, I'd stop feeling bad.

I left Dr. Eissler's bookish solitude without having dared to ask my questions—the man seemed so frail—but rejoicing: *I Have Spoken to Kurt Eissler, Who Sits at the Right Hand of God.*

Why I thought Sternbach would be impressed eludes me. He was, but not in the way I expected—not "my goodness! You are now hobnobbing with the best!"

"Eissler is an old man—he can hardly walk!" grumbled Sternbach. Who was even older.

Eissler's degree of renown then *really* dawned on me. I'd sat in his book-frenzied office, lined with his own volumes about Freud, Leonardo da Vinci, Viktor Tausk. I'd watched the white-haired figure putting aside his cane, painstakingly dictating a letter. I'd walked down his long hallway of empty rooms, and I'd thought, *Lonely.*

Sternbach wasn't lonely. He had *me.* But I was feeling worse than I had twenty-odd years before. Every session, I lay on the couch filled with the longing to speak and be heard while he rambled on about Vienna or lambasted my adolescent failures. After my fifty-minute hour, I routinely felt as though I'd been run over by a truck, but I believed I was being cured in the only possible way. People put up with chemotherapy, after all: it makes you feel and look rotten, but your cancerous tumors shrink.

I wonder if there's some other psychoanalysis out there, one in which the analyst sits back, lets the patient talk, putting in a word here and there as a helpful guide, the Virgil to Dante wandering through the Underworld. I asked a friend who'd often told me Dr. Sternbach's remarks "didn't sound like something an analyst would say" about her own analysis, which she'd undergone around the same time as I was slogging through mine. Her former analyst belongs to the 82nd Street temple, the New York Psychoanalytic Institute, the highest of the high.

We were in a Chinese restaurant eating something garlicky and delicious. She sighed, sipped her tea, thought about it. Her analysis hadn't involved any bullying, she said. "It was on the whole interesting and gave me insight into my upbringing, but I think it just went on too long, ten years, and I wonder how much good it really did me, as I now tend not to think about bad things I don't want to deal with. I think it left me with a sense of wanting to avoid too much introspection." She shrugged. "Now the stuff I talked about just seems like the stuff you go through in your twenties, whether you're talking to an analyst or not."

We sat there, two ladies pushing sixty, thinking that over, me wishing I had my twenties back. I would have preferred to make my own mistakes rather than embark upon a course of study—a PhD in English—for which I was completely unsuited. I'd dog-paddled my way through Columbia, and although I like teaching literature, the agonizing ten years spent in graduate school, wishing I could take dance classes but thinking I should put childish things behind me, weren't worth the experience. I would have enjoyed being a moderately successful dancer. Today, I tap dance—I've performed with an amateur group. My Svengali years lasted all too long, but my current high at being released from the prison of Sternbach's endless needs has never really diminished. This bird has flown.

Josef and I will soon celebrate our twentieth wedding anniversary, and the stability of our union is inversely proportionate to our geographical distance from my mother. Although she's ninety-six, Mom retains every last marble, handwriting lengthy letters about "these old people" in her assisted living facility, who eat with their eyes shut or have special friends. Mom dines with "cute little old ladies," she writes. "Imagine!" she adds. "I sit with a 107-year-old woman. She has dinner with a 100-year-old man."

These cris de coeur detailing her noblesse oblige arrive weekly. Sometimes daily.

"I think of myself as 'normal' and everyone else is just a bit odd," she writes, so that I can praise her. "That's life in Antiquity Haven."

When I visit, the nurses say, "Oh, your mother is wonderful! Such a gem!"

But there are things only a daughter sees—or feels. Like Mom's hugs, which I've learned to avoid, especially on train platforms. On one occasion, she thrust her pelvis into mine, gazing brightly at me as if she had no idea what she was doing, and let's not tell, shall we?

I was expecting—or rather, to be honest, wishing for—a warm hug, and what I got fell into no category recognized by polite society. She gazed penetratingly into my eyes, the sweetest, most giving little girl in the world—couldn't I see love in her limpid blue eyes that were staring into mine? Why was I lowering my own eyes and not gazing directly into hers?

It's just that you want to eat me alive, Mom, is what I think. What I don't say out loud.

But I wouldn't hurt a fly, is the message broadcast by those wide eyes that make me think of Alfred Hitchcock at his most terrifying. *She loves to see me—in nightmares, she's out in the garden staring through my window desperately as I dress. I see her eyes, grab a robe to cover myself, and open a window to demand why she's standing outside looking at me. She vanishes. She never wanted me to know she was there.*

If a small child hugged me in that demanding, rapacious way, naked need for attention announcing itself, I'd not feel surprised. I'd expect—and be delighted by—my husband possessively sweeping his groin against mine. Mom's hug vied for both categories, and I extricated myself as soon as I could.

Just prior to my most recent visit, she escaped her diligent nurses, who have no legal authority to restrain her, and taxied to the Back Bay station. There she stood, shivering in a thin cotton blouse as I stepped off the train—it was April, and cold in Boston—in my shearling coat. She moved toward me with remarkable speed for an elderly lady as I whipped off my coat and said, "Here, Mom! You must be freezing!" Like a torero facing a bull's horns, I whirled my coat around her shuddering shoulders, managing to avoid, this time, the hug. She wagged her head back and forth, frowning, an angry four-year-old, and complained, in her little-girl voice, "Oh, I have to do what *you* say!"

I smiled. "I have a heavy sweater, see?" I did. She kept the coat on but wanted to haul my suitcase, all but stamping her foot when I took it myself.

By this time, I'd already wished I could just go home instead of completing the visit that seemed obligatory, and was planned to continue through the following afternoon. I was relieved to find that the "guest room" at the assisted living facility had a lock and key.

Even so, I rolled my suitcase against the door.

ACKNOWLEDGMENTS

I have to start with the late lamented: Julia C. Schieffelin and Ruth Carpenter offered the feeling I had something to say—they encouraged me to write and gave me the all-important insight that all writing begins with an idea. They helped me articulate thoughts and never seemed to mind when these emerged in less than ideal form. Elizabeth Hardwick's acid wit and precisely tailored quotations jump-started my writing. For me, she provided a few lines from Nathanael West: "It is hard to laugh at the need for beauty and romance, no matter how tasteless, even horrible, the results of that need are. But it is easy to sigh. Few things are sadder than the truly monstrous." Ms. Hardwick knew both that I longed for beauty and romance and that I wanted to write about the truly monstrous.

In the land of the living: Elizabeth Dalton's writing class, which demanded what initially seemed an insurmountable forty pages of work in a single semester, taught me that quantity eventually becomes quality. Over the last forty years, she has continued to offer lengthy, insightful critiques, and I'm very grateful.

Members of my former writer's group— Mark Alpert, Dave King, Steve Goldstone, Eva Mekler, and Catherine Hiller— thank you for all your help and support over the years.

Lisa Ohlen Harris, editor extraordinaire, invested an enormous amount of thought and time—way above and beyond the call of duty—in my writing and helped me to understand both the story I was telling and the best way to tell it. The book would never have materialized without Lisa's help.

Danu Morrigan, your website made sense of so much in my life. Thank you.

Tanja Brachaczek, thank you for asking me, "What are you feeling right now?" Here is your answer.

I have to thank my parents and my brother for a memorable life, which taught me the importance of observation.